Laura G. Collins

By-gone Tourist Days

Letters of Travel

Laura G. Collins

By-gone Tourist Days
Letters of Travel

ISBN/EAN: 9783337136864

Printed in Europe, USA, Canada, Australia, Japan

Cover: Foto ©Andreas Hilbeck / pixelio.de

More available books at **www.hansebooks.com**

By-gone Tourist Days
Letters of Travel

By LAURA G. COLLINS
Author of "Immortelles and Asphodels"

ILLUSTRATED

"I consider letters the most vital part of literature"
—*Elizabeth Barrett Browning*

CINCINNATI
THE ROBERT CLARKE COMPANY
1900

INSCRIPTION.

Respectfully inscribed to the dear friends to whom the letters were written, and by them preserved.

CONTENTS.

LONDON LETTER—April 7, 1882, . . . 1
   Trip on the Atlantic—The Steamer Adriatic—Storm on the Ocean—Chester—English Cathedrals—To Liverpool—Chatsworth—Stratford—The 318th Anniversary of Shakespeare—Oxford—Magdalen College—"Addison's Walk"—New College—Sir Joshua Reynolds-Window—At Warwick—Bodlean Library—Ashmolean Museum—Spofford Brooks and Canon Liddon.

LONDON LETTER—June 11, 1882, . . . 16
   Seeing London—Advantage of being in a great city—The boarding-house, just for Americans—Windsor Palace—Gray's grave—Moncure Conway—Canon Farrar—Bostonians—American Cousins—From London on the way to Scotland.

FROM LONDON TO EDINBURGH—July 4, 1882, 22
   Four hours at York—The Nuns of St. Leonard's Hospital—St. Mary's Abbey—"The Five Sisters"—Newcastle-on-Tyne—Durham—The Cathedral—St. Cuthbert—The Tomb of Bede—The Legend of Bede—Wandering minstrels—Scenery on the route—The sunset—A Scotch lady—List of tourists.

SCOTLAND LETTER—July 21, 1882, . . 32
   Edinburgh—Holyrood Palace—Castle with relics of Mary Queen of Scots—Alexander Swift says—Of traveling—Dumfermline—The Abbey of Robert Bruce—Newbattle Abbey.

CONTENTS.

HEIDELBERG LETTER—August 16, 1882, . . 38
  In Heidelberg—The Neckar—The places I have been—Sketches over the line of travel—The scenes visited from England to Heidelberg.

HEIDELBERG LETTER—September 3, 1882, . 41
  Heidelberg; this is home—From Nuremberg—The enchantment and charms of the old city—The streets, buildings, bridges, churches, museums and galleries—Masterpieces of Durer, Kraft, Stoss and Vischer—The works of numerous artists—The lime tree—The lamp that has been lighted since 1326—The crown princess—The Exposition—Going back some day—A day of rest—Cape Colony English ladies—My traveling companion.

BADEN-BADEN—September 19, 1882, . . . 44
  Heidelberg on the Neckar—The castle, the Jettenbühl—"Das Grosse Fass"—Mapping out Switzerland—The floods—In the Gardens—The Black Forest—The Oos—The trees on the banks—To Strassburg.

NUREMBERG—September 27, 1883, . . . 47
  From Heidelberg to Nuremberg—Nuremberg the objective point—Ancestors back to 1570—Up the Neckar—The scenery—Two historic points—Hotels full—Grand Exposition—Superb attractions—Old lime tree—Durer's monument—The princess and family—A wedding—Traveling alone—German lady—At Baden—Friedrichsbad—The days at Strassburg.

MUNICH LETTER—September 24, 1882, . . 60
  Old and New Schloss—Trinkhalle and its waters—The great Friedrichsbad—Strassburg Cathedral—The wonderful clock—St. Thomas Church, with monument to Marshal Saxe—The Strassburg specialty, pâtés-de-foisgras—The attractive city, Constance—Monastery where

CONTENTS.   ix

Huss was imprisoned—The place where Jerome suffered sentence—From Constance to Lindau—The beauty of country and scenery—The Alps again—Words not equal to doing justice—Innumerable places of attraction—München, the capital of little Bavaria.

MÜNCHEN LETTER—October 11, 1882, . . 64
Visit to royal palace—A woman's voice in American English—Walks and drives around Munchen—Looking in the shop windows—Picking up pictures—Call at the book-store—"The Last Judgment," largest oil painting in the world—Other pictures and sketches—Vesper service—Munich a large city—Neighbors—A Prussian officer.

MUNICH LETTER—November 18, 1882, . . 77
Letters, letters, letters—An evening with friends—My husband and early childhood—Happy days—Dear hills, beautiful hills, sacred hills—Youthful days—The house where I was born—"The Point"—That "exuberant set"—Another Mrs. C.—Bavarian officer—Anticipation of seeing the Alps—A concert—Booth—Letters.

MÜNCHEN LETTER—November 20, 1882, . . 87
A homesick heart—The leaf from a tree—Views about the old homestead—The royal family at church—Royal dames—One of the princesses, a beautiful woman—The king—The music—The church—My religion.

MUNICH LETTER—December 12, 1882, . . 92
Repetition—Letter of the "altogethery type"—My style—Love, late in life—Indian summer—"That vale of Aberdeen"—Beautiful old ladies—That singular death-bed speech—The divine musician—French books—Dutch reading—The epic, Nibelungenlied—The king's palace.

CONTENTS.

MUNICH LETTER—December 22, 1882, . . 100
My counterfeit presentment—The crayon portrait—"Paint me as I am"—About my pictures—The home of my childood—"The Place of Roses"—Les Petites Miseres de la vie Conjugale—Christmas coming—What John did—Christmas, Christmas.

MUNICH LETTER—January 2, 1883, . . . 105
Preparations for Christmas—Bavaria and its kings—The public buildings—Music—The house of Wittelsbach dates from 1110—The Maximilians—The king on his death-bed—The present king, Ludwig II—His character—His royal palaces—The Gallery of Ancestors—The king a poet—His refined taste—The king's spotless reputation—Of the kings.

MÜNCHEN LETTER—January 15, 1883, . . 117
Christmas and New Years—The scathingest tongue—Christmas tree—The Nibelungenlied in German—Church services—German New Year's Eve—Our frau's banquet.

MUNICH LETTER—October 4, 1886, . . . 126
Of writing letters—Ingenious sophism—The little girl that prayed—The readable letter with a secret—His age—Miss B——'s letter—A grand gala day—Sunday the open day—The king—Royal family—Royal personages—Officers of state—A four o'clock tea.

PARIS LETTER—February 4, 1883, . . . 134
At last in Paradise—From Munich to Paris—The journey a dream—One's own vernacular—View from my private balcony—In sight of the Mackey's palace—Grace Greenwood in Paris—What an enchantment to know places by sight—The street scenes—Vast concourse of seething humanity—The weather—The flowers.

CONTENTS.   xi

PARIS LETTER—February 8, 1883,   .   .   . 137
   To begin—Figures—Not writing for fame or filthy lucre—
   "Two in one existence"—From Munich to Paris alone
   —The experience of cold—The German cars comfort-
   able—Fallen in love—Paris, London and Munich Com-
   pared—Manufactory of the Gobelins—Pompeian palace
   —Viewing art—Language—Night—Solitude—To Italy
   from Paris.

PARIS LETTER—September 1, 1883, .   .   . 144
   In Paris again after six months—Good intentions—Feminine interruption—A flash of inspiration—The lion of
   sandstone carved in a grotto—Trip to the glaciers—First
   mule ride—Return from the sublime spectacle—The descent more difficult than the ascent—English ladies—
   From Interlaken to Bern—Lake Leman—The Garden
   in which Gibbon wrote the conclusion of his great
   work—Chillon—Passage to Chamony—All the way to
   Geneva—That book—The Pension—The Madame.

PARIS LETTER—Januaay 1, 1884,   .   .   . 158
   Letter—Verses—Christmas Eve—Tree party—My hostess
   and myself—Salutatory an impromptu poem—The eve-
   ning's entertainment—Twelfth Night—I shun sleep—
   "Characteristics"—Sending the book—A letter from
   Miss B.—The article on Burns—Finis and reflections.

PARIS LETTER—April 1, 1884, ... 166
   Enjoying Paris in fair weather—President Grevy—The
   numerous entertainments—There is no hostess—The
   musical side of Paris—A pleasant American family—
   Sunday afternoon concert—The music—The audience—
   To the Luxembourg with an American girl.

PARIS LETTER—December 6, 1885,   .   .   . 169
   Letter acknowledged—I am again a wandering star—The

xii   CONTENTS.

   delights of travel—The poor king who lost his head—
   Thomas a Becket—Whitehall—Government buildings—
   Saw Gladstone's and Salisbury's seats—Went to Temple
   Bar—Old clocks—The cathedral—Vespers at Little St.
   Martin's—Crossed the Channel—Sight-seeing—Cuvier
   and Humboldt—Experiences, drives and sights—Pleasant people we met.

PARIS LETTER—December 13, 1886, . . . 175
   Return delayed by storms—Miss B—— came from Sweden
   —Proposed trip on the Nile—A line from under old
   Cheops.

PARIS LETTER—March 8, 1887, . . . 177
   Disappointed about the Jerusalem trip—Contributions
   from every grand division—No date for sailing—Ladies
   from Louisville, Ky.—The title of the little book—
   Madame gives a house-warming—Bloom and beauty.

PARIS LETTER—April 26, 1887, . . . 180
   Birthday anniversary—Dispensations of conscientiousness
   —How the days go—The sight-seeing never comes to an
   end—The "Salon" open for the Annual Exposition—
   At the Exposition—Numerous pictures—"Theodora,"
   Sara Bernhardt's great character—Two French ladies—
   The musical entertainment given me—Paris in the
   month of May.

PARIS LETTER—May 29, 1887, . . . 185
   The letter and the book—Figures and a woman's age—
   Pictures—Millet's "L'Angelus"—Subjects and character of paintings—"The little book"—The drive—
   Champs Elysées as a fashionable resort—The enchantment of the scenes—"The little book" again, and
   again.

CONTENTS. xiii

VENICE LETTER—June 8, 1883, . . . 192
    The letter in fancy from Florence—No rules from the flight of imagination—Longfellow says it for me—Venice in June—Drifting about in a gondola—The Grand Canal—The dazzling glory of the scene—A trance; a dream; perfect, perfect Venice!—Allusion to a story of life—A book to come forth—If I am to die to-morrow . . . —The ideal woman and friend—Kentucky gossip—Oh! oh! oh! perfect, perfect Venice!

LUCERNE LETTER—June 26, 1883, . . . 201
    The wooden horse of Donatello—Goethe's palm tree—From Padua to Verona—Juliet's tomb—The house of Capulets—Milan—The cathedral—Grand Victor Emanuel Gallery—Pictures in galleries—Visit to libraries—View of levées—Italian lakes and scenes—The tropical bloom—Nightingale songs—The grand climb up the Alps—The glaciers—Snow flower, edelweiss—The ruins of castles—The moonlight scene—The descent from the Alps—The aching heart, like the dying gladiator.

VIENNA LETTER—October 17, 1883, . . . 214
    No end to the beginning—The opera—Letters—The surface of things—Below the surface—Knowledge of more breadth—My hostess—Wagner's operas—The object of my pilgrimage to Vienna—The aurist of Europe—The specialist's quarters—The Imperial Library.

SIENA LETTER—March 4, 1883, . . . 224
    Things we saw on the way—Shrine of Petrarch's Laura—The Papal palaces—The frescoes—Musee Calvet—Vernet Gallery and pictures—The moonlight drive to Marseilles—At Cannes—An English lady—Hotel on the sea-front—The moonrise out of the sea—Bishop Littlejohn, of Rhode Island—A tram-drive—Excursion to Monaco and Monte Carlo—Pisa—Geneva—Mt. Blanc.

xiv CONTENTS.

ROME LETTER—March 19, 1883, . . . 231
An Ohioan from Granville—Naples and views—Museums and the palace of Capodimonte—Picture of Michael Angelo and Vittoria Colonna—Pompeian frescoes—Vittoria Colonna's husband—Vesuvius at night—Longfellow's poem, "Amalfi"—Paestum—Ideal drive—Museum—Narcissus listening to Echo—Palm Sunday at St. Peter's—The Sistine Chapel—Goethe's words—Hawthorne's Rome—The Marble Faun—Springtime—Christmas flowers—Christmas souvenirs.

ROME LETTER—April 4, 1883, . . . 238
Scenes along the coast of Italy—Little villages—The mountains—Monastery of the Capuchins—The macaroni factory—The monastery and monks—Our Paestum day—Vesuvius before the charmed gaze—Birthplace of Tasso—Celebrated places—Second trial of Naples—Trip from Naples to Rome—Ancient Capua—Monte Casino, its associations—Rome—Palm Sunday—Various services—English lady—Holy Week—Drive on the Via Appia—The Catacombs and tombs—The grotto—The tree of Numa's wisdom.

ROME LETTER—April 24, 1883, . . . 251
Importance of address in a foreign land—Guercino's fresco of Aurora—Scene in Imperial Rome—"Rome mistress of the world"—Story of Eve—Tasso memorial room—Swarm of lizards—A view of St. Peter's—Pompey's statue—The Plaza—The Jews' quarters, called Ghetto—The house of Rienzi—Protestant cemetery—Burial place of Keats and the heart of Shelley.

ROME LETTER—May 2, 1883, . . . 261
"While Rome stands, the world stands"—The rounds of churches—The galleries and museums—Palaces and shops—"Being in Rome, do as Romans do"—Piazzi di

CONTENTS.

San Giovanni, the largest in existence—One of the eleven obelisks—Mosaic frescoes—The queen in her carriage—Church of St. Onafrio, on the Janiculus—The three frescoes by Domenichino and Leonardo da Vinci—Tasso buried here—Three churches of the Aventine—Galleries—Artists' quarters—Our Rodgers and Ives—Their art—Italian artist—Dwight Benton, formerly of Cincinnati, Ohio—Italian scenes.

MAIORI LETTER—April 5, 1886, . . . 274
Apology for delinquent letter—"What a butterfly she is!"—One of the party sick—On the Mediterranean—Longfellow's poem—The steep climb—The poor little donkey—Features of the scene—"The death in life"—The region abounds in drives—Talk of Sicily and Africa—A letter—The sacred few . . .—The little book—Blessed be the potato, henceforth and forever!

NAPLES LETTER—May 1, 1886, . . . 281
A drive to Salerno—From there to Paestum—The temple of Neptune—An incident of missing glasses—Return to Salerno—Then to Pompeii—Naples—Friends from Tunis—A steamer for Sicily—Storm at sea—Palermo, its environs—The palaces—The drives and places we visited—The museum, Metopes, and splendid art—Beauty of the country—The fountain of Arethusa—Roman amphitheater—The quarries—Mt. Etna—The seven rocks of Cyclops—Messina—That coat of arms of Sicily—The heart-ache of good-byes.

LAUTERBRUNNEN LETTER—July 29, 1886, . 291
Wrought up over letters—"Poaching on your preserves"—The cause of wit—Friends, their character estimated—Of writing—Sojourn in the beautiful valley—The Staubach—The Jungfrau.

EGYPT LETTER—December 30, 1886, . . 295
  Aboard steamer Prince Abbas—On the Nile—"In the teeth of a storm"—Sunrise and sunset on the Mediterranean—Acquaintances, a citizen from the "hub"—At Alexandria—The seven wonders—To Cairo—English officers—The Pyramids—Pillars at Heliopolis—"The Virgin's tree"—The island of Rhodda—Mosques and tombs—The site of Memphis—"Twelve miles of wonderland—The air—The flowers—The guests on steamer—One can live too much in books.

EGYPT LETTER FROM PARIS—February 10, 1887, 302
  Agreeable surprises—Down the Nile—The atmosphere and mysterious influence of scene—Landing of steamer—Our donkey ride—The tombs—The imposing magnificence of the monuments—Rain in Egypt—Reflections—Pictures to help tell the story—The coming book.

CUBA LETTER—April 7, 1885, ... 307
  The magical isle of Cuba—Tropical vegetation—Sunrise in the harbor of Havana—The trip on the steamer—Moro Castle—Strange scene on landing—The buildings—The drive, atmosphere and scenery—The watch incident—Shopping expedition—People we met—To Cerro—Sugar plantations and process of sugar-making—The caves—The beautiful island, Cuba—The freedom of slaves—Spanish government.

A VISION OF FATIGUE, ... 322

LIST OF ILLUSTRATIONS.

	PAGE
Shakespeare's Birthplace, from below, Stratford,	11
Room in Shakespeare's Home, Stratford,	12
Mary, Queen of Scots, Edinburgh,	32
Pension and Garden to which Goethe wrote a Poem, Heidelberg,	38
The Old Kaiser at Historical Window,	71
Louis II, the Mad King of Bavaria,	90
Queen Louise,	126
The Historic Windmill,	131
The Old Lion, Lucerne,	147
The Old Lion at the Arsenal, Venice,	192
Lord Byron's Palace, Venice,	196
Pantheon, Rome,	242
Strada dei Sepolcri (Street of Tombs), Pompeii,	248
Quirinal, Rome,	259
Naples, General View,	281
Peasant Cart, Palermo,	283
Interior of Museum, Palermo,	285
Archimedes,	288
Head of Medusa, Palermo,	290

LETTER FROM ENGLAND.

WHERE to begin? That is the question. The ideas, thoughts, feelings, come, not in battalions, but like the hosts of Alexander, or our own, in "the late unpleasantness," or like the bubbles in the foam on the crests of the waves "a moment here, then gone forever." I am wishing for the arms of Briareus, with their hundred hands, to help catch and fix them on the page. Such a trip! The Atlantic was never known to exhibit such a peculiar turbulence of waves and water generally. The steamer Adriatic (in which we sailed April 6th) kept up such a lurching and pitching as I never had an idea of before. One day it was impossible for me to keep my feet, and after trying in vain to dress in the morning, I retired to my berth. But it was as much as the sailors could do to keep their feet, and three were badly hurt. How my friends would have laughed, could they have seen my frantic struggles to accomplish a toilette. The two "steamer trunks" and our hand satchels were chasing each other all around me, and knocking wildly from one side to the other, and I in the midst, shooting and slipping, clutching and grabbing, wildly, frantically, at doors, berth and washstand. But I was so glad not to be seasick, I didn't mind anything else much.

One spectacle of this turbulence in the "r-r-r-rolling forties," as the chambermaid called our bearing (I wish I could give that whirr of her r s), was of peculiar and extraordinary sublimity and uniqueness. It kept me at my porthole for I know not how long. The steamer was sweeping right along in an immense hollow, or crater as it were, in the ocean, and in which was comparative calm. Afar off the water rose in encircling ranges of vast mountains—"Alps upon Alps"—capped with white foam. From these snowy cones, like the eruptions of volcanoes, burst forth in swift succession great columns of the seething mass that shot upward apparently to the very heavens and exploded.

I did not know at the time that this was unusual, but in speaking of it afterwards found it had not been observed by the other passengers —all or the most of whom were seasick—nor have I since met with any traveler who had ever seen it; nor read any description of it.

We had a lovely Easter Sunday on the broad Atlantic. The captain presented me with two Easter eggs prepared expressly for me as a testimonial of my good seamanship. I was never seasick. The device was a white star and the name of the steamer—Adriatic. I was the only lady thus honored. We had a pleasant company: R. H. Dana and his wife (a daughter of Longfellow), two charming ladies, relatives of Longfellow, a Unitarian minister and his young sister, all from Boston; and a Mrs. Blake, from Canada. These were the parties we saw the most of, except Mrs. Dana, who was not well. Mr. Dana was one of the most attractive and interesting persons I ever met, the kind that has the effect of a flash of sunlight coming into a room. One of the ladies was a Unitarian, and that brought us together. The minister was going to attend a Unitarian conference of the English Unitarian Church, which met at Liverpool, April 18th. She and I constituted ourselves delegates at large, and decided to attend. We landed Sunday, the 16th, remained till afternoon, attending church at an old cathedral of some note; then lunching at the Northwestern Hotel, and away we came to Chester.

How much do you know about Chester?

I'll take for granted all its history. The "old cathedral city" and the "old walled city" is the way the guide-books speak of it. I walked its two miles of wall, well-preserved, picturesque, and commanding lovely views. I mounted one of the towers on it, called King Charles the First's, because from it he watched the fatal progress of the battle of Rowton Moor. I looked out of the very queer little windows from which he watched. The old woman who shows it is as bright and keen of tongue, if not as incisive, as Mrs. Poyser. She said she liked Americans, and always enjoyed their visits, and that they paid her every year a most extraordinary honor. "Just think of a whole country celebrating your birthday! Wouldn't you feel honored? That's what you Americans do." She said it with mischievous, snapping eyes. Of course I took in in a moment that the Fourth of July was her birthday. "Ah," I replied, " and to think of fifty millions of people doing all that honor, and not knowing what they are doing." "Fifty millions of people!" She came right up to me, and her look changed to amazement—"what a grand country it must be!" I told her it was too bad her name was unknown, and she must give it to me. "Mary Huxley." I said,

> "Why, Mary Huxley, you've a very good name,
> And I'm sure I think it a crying shame
> That it is not better known to fame."

You ought to have seen her delight. She talked to me down to the very last step, after giving me "a hearty grip" by way of good-bye.

Then I saw Chester Cathedral, where Hugh Lupus, nephew of William the Conqueror, is buried. On Sunday night, some of us attended service there, after which there was an organ recital, a very fine performance. Next morning, all five of us went down into the dark, damp, crypts. The amount of exquisite carving in it is something wonderful. I am not going into the age and size of it and all that. Go to the library and get a book on English Cathedrals and Cathedral Towns and read, and think that that is what your correspondent is seeing. Another one is St. John's Church, still more ancient, with its abbey, a lovely ivy-covered ruin. I could not bear to leave it. Another feature is the old castle now used as an armory and barracks. The hands of the Romans have left many evidences of their work here in the wall, the columns still standing in place of some kinds of fortifications. The old town is full of queer things, and has a wierd sort of fascination; among these "the Rows," a succession of arcades built on the roofs of ancient triangular-shaped houses. The handsomest shops are in them. The neighborhood has the honor of containing Eaton Hall, the seat of the Duke of Westminster. We visited it, driving and walking all over its splendid walks, and gardens, and lawns, and parks, and getting a first-rate look into the palace. We could not go inside, because it was full of workmen finishing the inside ornamentation. The grounds are ten square miles in extent. There were immense conservatories, full of the rarest flowers and plants. In one I saw the Egyptian lotus floating in full bloom in an immense tank. The head gardener was our guide. He was a very intelligent person, well-mannered and pleasant and clever, because he gave me a handful of flowers and broke off a nice little branch from a cedar of Lebanon, brought from the Holy Land expressly for the place. He gave us a great deal of information about the family; among other things he told me the Duke was not handsome, but a good man. He spoke with emphasis.

The Dee winds through those miles of acres and is spanned by a number of bridges. The villages of the tenantry are pretty and looked comfortable. I saw deer by hundreds in the park. We returned to Liverpool, and remained two days in attendance on the conference. A number of the leading men were there, and we heard them speak and preach. There were Armstrong, Carpenter, Sir Thomas Hayward and others. They were fine-looking men, and extremely interesting. The audience was as enthusiastic and demonstrative as that of our Methodist Conferences.

From Liverpool we whisked away to Rowsley Station, Derbyshire, to the Peacock Inn, the quaintest manor-house, now doing duty according to its name. The object of this was to visit Chatsworth, the seat of the Duke of Devonshire, and Haddon Hall, a lovely unused ruin, belonging to the Duke of Rutland. The country in every direction was a vision of beauty—a sea of living green—bespangled with flowers as thickly as the floor of heaven is inlaid with stars; or in Derbyshire, breaking up into great cliffs, showing the beautiful stone which is so generally used in building. The grounds of the inn were washed by the Derwent, a winding stream of exceeding beauty.

We made an early start in a wagonette for Chatsworth. It was an ideal day—the Spring in full burst, with that delicate film of blue mist that always makes me think of a veil, to enhance its charms—the whole way a succession of pictures—vales, swelling uplands, far hills, the Derwent in its curious curves. We were speechless and exclamatory by turns.

Chatsworth is a palace, in the midst of its thousands of acres cultivated and adorned in every possible way; its exquisite lawn laid out in innumerable gardens in Italian, Alpine, German, French, and ever so many other styles; its wonderful conservatory designed by Sir Joshua Paxton, who modeled the Crystal Palace on the same plan, as you no doubt know; and the gorgeousness of the long suite of show rooms. The rooms of course are filled with all that the money and taste of its long generations have accumulated—the rooms in themselves, for their noble dimensions, rich, tasteful and expensive finish; and their lovely views of stream, lakes, meadows, forests, and lovely distances. I saw the hangings of a state bedstead worked by Mary Queen of Scots, and the Countess of Shrewsbury; the rosary of Henry the Eighth; and some portraits of the beautiful duchesses that have distinguished the house (though not Georgiana); and some splendid pieces of statuary. I shall never forget Canova's Endymion, and Thorwalsden's Venus. The guide went round the grounds by my side and proved himself a most agreeable fellow—telling me all the family gossip I cared to know. I dare not attempt to get it all in here, though I've a misgiving you'd rather hear it than all the rest. I may as well tell you that I always keep close to the guide and—it pays. They are always the head, or one of the gardeners, and are a constant astonishment to me for their good manners, choice language, as well as their intelligence.

I asked if the heir, the Marquis of Hartington (leader in the House of Commons), was handsome; he laughed merrily, shaking his head, "No indeed, he is very plain, and you just ought to see him slouch around here. This is the way he walks"—and he gave an illustration to my infinite amusement. Only he and I were together, the rest were lagging a wide interval behind.

The deer park has two thousand acres and eight hundred head of deer. We saw several different herds of one hundred each, perhaps two hundred.

Next by a short drive, to Haddon Hall on

a hill overlooking as fair a scene as eye would care to dwell on. A soft drab stone, time-stained and worn, moss and ivy covered, it is an immense pile built around a quadrangular court, with its ancient rooms sufficiently well-preserved to show in what state it was kept away back in that romantic age. The grand banqueting hall, with antlers for ornaments, its old table in the upper end, with the same old benches, both worm-eaten; besides this the dining hall for daily use, wainscoted to the ceiling in heavy, dark oak panels, and a great round table; the drawing-room with its arras, hangings said to be of the fourteenth century, the bed-rooms hung in the same way; the dancing saloon one hundred and ten by seventeen feet wide, with its grand stained windows, and a bust of one of the countesses taken after her death. I went up Percival tower and stood on it looking down into the "inner court" (the quadrangle) and off over the landscape, and trying to imagine "the olden time." There is a door opening on to an avenue of yews with a terrace and steps into a walled flower garden with a postern gate in the wall, outside which are steps leading to a bridge across the moat beyond which lies an expanse of open meadow, and a pretty story

Shakespeare's Birthplace, from below, Stratford.

says the loveliest daughter of the house stole out this way to "off and away," with her "young Lochinvar," he and his steed awaiting her at the hither side of the bridge. The little boy who opened the postern for us, said in answer to us: "This is the gate, and them's the steps, and that are the bridge she crossed to the 'oss."

From the Peacock next a. m. to Stratford-on-Avon! Next day was Sunday, and the birthday of Shakespeare. Think of my spending it at his birthplace! It is almost too much to realize. The first afternoon we walked to see his birthhouse (just the outside), the hall where Garrick's present stands, and the bridge over the Avon from which is a pretty view of the church where he lies. The morning found us all fresh and ready for church. There was fine music and a full congregation. You know the whole service is intoned in the English Church. When the vicar went to his desk for that I dreaded to hear a word, fearing it would not be in harmony with the day. It proved to be the best sermon I ever heard from the Episcopal pulpit, indeed an inspiration. After the congregation was dismissed we asked permission to enter the chancel to see the grave, and I had a collection of the flowers he knew so well to lay upon it. It was "against rule" to let any one in at that hour, but the vicar instantly and courteously accorded us this as soon as he knew we were Americans. I knelt and laid the flowers by the inscription. The "painted bust" is just above the grave. I did not like it. It looked both beefy and beery. Too much so for my ideal of him who the vicar had just said "was the greatest poet and perhaps the greatest being that ever lived." It was the 318th anniversary. No wonder he chose "Trinity" for his last resting-place. It is a beautiful situation on the Avon, and from the street you walk up a long avenue of lime trees, on either side of which are the graves of centuries. We stayed three days at Stratford, and to-morrow we go, as the great Cardinal went, "by easy roads to Leicester;" we are going to London.

May 1st. We came here Saturday, after such a two days in that "ancient university city," Oxford, as I hope most fervently I shall repeat in extenso. It was from one extreme enjoyment to something beyond! I stepped into the university founded by Alfred the Great, a huge mass of time-stained and somewhat crumbling marble. I went through Christ College, first into the kitchen. "The very best time you could

Room in Shakespeare's Home, Stratford.

have come," said the usher. Dinner was in full progress! The room is a cube of forty feet. Such a baronial banquet preparation I never saw. The oldest relic is the door leading into the court, where the fuel is kept, heavy, black, battered, iron-bound oak. From the kitchen to the refectory, with its splendid array of pictures. Going out under the tower, we heard "old Tom" ring out the hour in his sonorous tones. To Magdalen College to see the chapel with its wonderful immense window in brown sepia, three hundred years old, representing the day of judgment, and its reredos extending from the floor to the ceiling and from side wall to side wall. Then to "Addison's Walk," the loveliest, most sequestered, serpentine, and then long great vista of greenery, bound on either side by lovely streams and wide meadows edged with pollard willows. To New College, with its rival chapel and great window, designed by Sir Joshua Reynolds, representing Faith, Hope, and all the virtues mentionable. Anything more exquisite than Hope was never fashioned by man. The window is made, it is said, of the finest stained glass in the world. We passed by the church where Amy Robsart lies. At Warwick we saw the magnificent tomb of her cruel earl, and the effigy of himself and third wife, carved and colored, reposing thereupon. On to the Bodleian Library, with its treasures of books, rare old manuscripts, ancient illuminated works; I can't enumerate its treasures, but one of the most curious and interesting was some papyrus rolls from Herculaneum, showing the scorch. Its picture gallery was a perfect fascination, with its portraits and busts of a long array of historical persons whom we have admired, reverenced, loved, and hated, all our lives. It was all an aggravating rush from one thing to another, that one wanted to hang over and study and steep the whole being in. I would go to the Ashmolean Museum to see a few things—Alfred's jewel, a priceless treasure, the chatelaine watch of Queen Elizabeth, in turquoise and gold, with the chain formed of charms in different devices—two of hair. I wondered if either was her own. Cromwell's watch right beside hers, heavy, thick, not very large, but looking as if it was meant to stand all the battering of the man's career. One of the most interesting of all the personal trifles—shall I call them?—was a kind of charm worn by John Hampden in the civil war. This was the motto:

"Against my king I do not fight,
But for my king and kingdom's right."

There is not a spot in Oxford that is not enchanting. We staid at the "Mitre Hotel," the oldest house in the city. Our room was wainscoted to the ceiling, which was divided into three compartments by rich and pretty panels in rich flowers. I did not like to leave it, though walking its floors was a feat of dexterity worthy of being chronicled, they were so sunken and irregular. We came whizzing through the loveliest lowland country, saw Windsor in a misty veil of light rain, and all at once we were in Paddington Station, in the cab, rolling through London streets and directly at our boarding house. We are delightfully situated. Sunday morning we heard Spofford Brooks. He is just across the street. In the afternoon I went to St. Paul's to hear Canon Liddon. I was all eyes, if not ears. That splendid pile swallowed me up, mind, body and soul. And now with the din and clatter of four female tongues sounding in my ears, I will close this rambling epistle.

L. G. C.

Grosvenor Hotel, Chester, April 17, 1882.

LETTER FROM LONDON.

I AM still in this grandest city of the globe. Every day seems a fresh era in life, each hour ushers in new and more delightful experiences. I am confirmed in my opinion that this "little island," but mighty kingdom of the earth, is to be more to me than all the rest, and that my plan to spend "the season" in London was the very best I could have had. Indeed that was the one feature of this trip entirely clear to me. For the rest, I had a general outline to make headquarters of each of the great art centers, and let the gods provide the goods. No doubt I shall adhere to this in a way. Governor Chamberlain, who was here last year in August, said he could not have believed it would make such a difference to be here "in the season." I think you know the months of May, June and July constitute that elect time. Well, I have had as perfect a time as one could have in my way. Of course, there is that other—that means being presented at court, and getting into society, the first being the easier of the two! I have not hankered after either. There are some whom I have long admired, it would be a beatitude to know, such as the Earl of Shaftsbury, now eighty-one, whose whole life has been devoted to good and noble works (just last Tuesday he presided at the opening of a bazaar in behalf of a benevolent project), and the Duke of Devonshire and his family, Gladstone, John Bright and such. Alas! "they are a pitch beyond my flight," and so I am content to let all go. What I have drunk deep of is the great institutions—churches, galleries, the Tower, Parliament houses, hospitals, etc.

The boarding house in which we are is kept by English people, just for Americans, and foreigners. English people do not board; it is not "good form" with them. The host, a very intelligent, affable gentleman, and his wife, a bright, kind, out-spoken lady, say "they have known no Americans that have seen London to such advantage." They evidently regard us with great respect.

Tuesday was a glorious day. We spent it at Windsor, were all over the palace shown to the public, on the terrace, saw the gorgeous Albert Mausoleum, and St. George's Chapel with its exquisite monument to Princess Charlotte, the most perfect piece of sculpture I ever saw, and also the touching monument to the Prince Imperial, with his recumbent statue on it, a good likeness in pure white marble. It seems to me quite probable, since seeing it, that Princess Beatrice may have been in love with him. From Windsor we drove through Eaton, and a beautiful English lane to Stoke Pogis to see Gray's grave and the church and graveyard of the "Elegy." The little church is the most exquisite little gem I ever saw. I wish I dared give you a full description of that day, but it would take a ream of paper.

Well, this is Sunday evening. I went to hear Moncure Conway this forenoon at his own chapel. I was so much interested, more than I have been by any one I have heard but Canon Farrar. You may have heard him when he preached in Cincinnati. You may not agree with or approve of his views, but one cannot help being greatly interested and instructed. He has a scholarly look—the bowed head, that trick caught by bending constantly over books and writing, and a lively, expressive countenance, the kind that shows the effect of constant association with high thoughts and noble sentiments and lofty aspirations. He is in the best sense a teacher. I saw Mr. and Mrs. Taft there, and my friend Miss —— cried out, "Don't you want to go back and speak to them?" As we were in our carriage, and it was raining, I concluded to forego the pleasure. They are on their way to Vienna. It is rather pleasant to know so many Americans are around, even if you don't get to speak to them. We have a fresh supply of Bostonians. They are all chattering round the fire like so many daws—my *companions du voyage* helping their level best. They come and go, come and go, all the time. We often find ourselves laughing at large parties—"Oh! look quick; there they are, another lot of our countryfellows." They go about in gangs and everybody seems to recognize them at once as "Americans." I can't tell how they, the English, know us; but it is very easy for us to distinguish them. Their voices and *pronunciation* are very markedly different. All have a kind of abdominal pitch and intoning that are very pronounced.

I have found some relatives here, people who settled in England two hundred years ago, when my branch of the family emigrated from Holland to America. They are as purely English as I am American, and this is the first meeting since the original separation. One of my newly-found cousins is in the Somerset House, where he has a government office, and he *would* show us "what it contained of interest." It is a government building, registering marriages, births, deaths, keeping records, etc. The way he made us skip round and up and down and through long corridors in upper stories, and deep down in almost the bowels of the earth, was good for our circulation if not for our feet. It was just going through a vast library, for all these things are kept in volumes bound in Russia leather and shelved and catalogued. He invited us for Tuesday evening to meet a party of relatives and special friends he wished me to know; so I am counting on something of an introduction to English life. Thereby is a romance, our meeting, etc.; but of this another time.

Well, our time is up, and on Wednesday I have arranged to leave for our Scottish tour. This takes up the eastern side of England, through York and Durham to Edinburgh, where we shall spend a week. Thence through the Tromcho* and lakes, Caledonia canal, Inverness and back to "Auld Reekie," where we shall excursion to Abbotsford, Jedburg, and next

* Trossachs.

LETTER FROM ENGLAND.

Glasgow and Ayr, and down through western England by the English lakes—Windermere, Coniston, etc., back to London. We may go to Wales, or leave that out for the present and go to the Isle of Wight, and so across the Channel to some place in Brittany or Normandy, where we have "booked" ourselves for a month.

L. G. C.

London, June 11, 1882.

FROM LONDON TO EDINBURGH.

WE LEFT London on the morning of the 14th, after a seven weeks' sojourn, and, I must say it, one of perfect delight and satisfaction. Old Londoners could not remember a more charming "season;" the weather called forth rapturous comments, the city was full of attractions, the best and at their best, a most fortunate conjunction; and "all the world" seemed peopling its palaces, crowding its hotels, thronging its temples of art and pleasure, and pushing its way through the packed streets, to enjoy them. Believe me, it took a stout wrench to break away from all that. But as we said to our hostess in response to her amiable urgency to detain us yet longer, "Dear Madam, how shall we 'see the world,' unless we 'move on'?"

A four hours' railway ride brought us to York, where we "stopped over" till next afternoon to see the Minster, the walls and the ruins of St. Leonard's Hospital and St. Mary's Abbey, and the ancient city "in toto." The sun shone for us in most lavish brilliancy, and we went after lunch to the Cathedral, spending an hour or more wandering "through it with the verger all to ourselves" (which we always account a peculiarly good piece of luck, as much interesting information is to be gained, when he can give you undivided attention).

We stood long before each of the great windows, too rapt in admiration, it must be confessed, to give due heed to the great budget of details our guide was so kindly pouring out for our benefit. The "Five Sisters" was the first that arrested us, consisting of five lancet-shaped lights, fifty-four feet high by thirty wide. It was presented by five maiden sisters, who worked the patterns first. They must have had a busy time of it, and I am glad I was not one of them, but am one who has had the privilege of enjoying their pious handiwork. Next the west and east windows, the first about the size of the "Five Sisters," the latter said to be the largest in the world. As to the exquisite beauty of each, that is unutterable. We lingered and loitered in nave and choir and transept, till long after the sun had set, and then walked back to our hotel, a palace fit for any queen this world has ever throned; the views from its great French plate glass windows Victoria might be glad to claim. The next morning we attended choral service, and gave the entire forenoon to that splendid seat of Episcopal magnificence. From there we went to the ruins, both being in the same inclosure, a large tract laid out in beautiful walks and far-stretching expanses of lawn, with clumps of trees here and there, and beds and borders of flowers. I wish I had time to tell you how old these crumbling structures are, and the various fortunes to which they have been subjected. Suffice it that both are older than the time of the Conqueror, which surely would seem ancient enough.

In the afternoon we were most reluctant to "stick to our program," and go on to Durham, but we did. We had a reminder of home on the way in an hour's stop at Newcastle-on-Tyne— as coal begrimed as Pittsburgh. I was glad to leave it behind, and find fresh, clean air coming into my lungs as it vanished from my sight. We ran into Durham in good time for a climb to its Cathedral, "unequaled in situation on a high hill." Again we had a verger all to ourselves, and he proved a fellow with some wit, with all his overwhelming "stock in trade" of cathedral knowledge in architecture.

I was so hoarse I could only croak, but too athirst for knowledge to let that hinder. So, as I said something to this effect, "Tell me about that—the book I have does not tell anything, though I got the best I could find"—with the most mischievous smile he burst out, "I think you got something worse, have n't you?" We were fast friends from that moment till I bowed "good-bye" next day—crossing his willing hand with the inevitable silver shilling. You have read all about this cathedral; that it is a splendid example of Norman, early English, transitional, and perpendicular styles in its different parts; that St. Cuthbert is its patron saint, and his bones rest here; maybe, remember how his monks

> "From sea to sea, from shore to shore,
> Seven years Saint Cuthbert bore.
> And after many wanderings past,
> He chose his lordly seat at last,
> Where his cathedral huge and vast
> Looks down upon the weir;
> There deep in Durham's gothic shade
> His reliques are in secret laid,
> But none may know the place."

That was long ago, and now even I "know the place." I stood upon the flagstones that covered it! Bede is buried there, so I have to tell you that I leaned upon his tombstone and read the inscription:

"Hac sunt in fossa Bedae venerabilis ossa,"

and recalled the story of the monk's worry over his hexameter, his lucky nap, and the opportune help of that convenient angel, who fixed it up "all right" while he slept the sleep of the righteous. I saw the carved image of the Dun Cow, from which it got its name. I am not so sure that legend is so familiar to you. It took hard work, innumerable questions, search and research, for me to get hold of it, quaint and simple as it is. In that seven years' quest for a resting-place for the corpse, the monks had stopped with it at a place called Ward Law, from which they could not move it, it seeming fastened to the ground. This set them all praying to know where they should take it. The answer to their prayer was, "Dunholme" (Durham). As they were searching about in great perplexity, they heard a woman, who was looking for her stray cow, call to her neighbor, asking if she had seen it. The cry back was: "She is at Dunholme." Behold! this quest was ended. And the cow is a beauty of the kind that makes one wish she could be driven home into his own pasture, to be "a possession forever." She stands sleek and serene in her niche in the outer wall, and seems to follow you with a watchful gaze as you pluck buttercups and clover-blooms, lineal descendants, beyond a doubt, of those on which her prototype fed in the spacious close beneath her.

We tarried atop that green hill and in those sacred precincts, till the fainter day that is far from twilight, though the sun is long gone, warned us of the late hour. Such an evening as we had in ancient Durham—"a dirty hole in general," as a little Scotch boy wrote of it in 1820. And a little American woman verifies it to-day. First, a street concert by Highlanders in full national costume, with their screeching bagpipes. They ended and vanished. Then came trooping by a large body of the Salvation Army, with their leader, a woman, facing her forces and keeping time with a stick to their singing. She looked like a wild creature, and the spectacle was one more conducive to speculation than to admiration. As their frantic strains died away in the distance, a sweet, clear-ringing child voice burst forth. It soared up to us like a lark,

"Singing as it soars and soaring as it sings."

We opened our windows and saw a young boy standing in the street alone and without any instrument, singing with an absorption that made him oblivious to his surroundings. He did not even notice the fall of the pennies for which he was singing, till a woman, who had stopped to hear him, gathered them up and put them into his hands.

We felt as if we were listening to an incipient Brignoli. He went too. At eleven o'clock, the daylight not yet merged in night, we fell asleep to harp music, played by a band of Gypsies in most picturesque garb. We hurried to the cathedral next morning for "choral service," and heard some fine music, which attuned us to our loitering among its ancient memorials. After some hours inside we came out into the lovely day, and strolled off for a walk. From the crest of the hill on which the cathedral is built to the water's edge its wooded sides are laid out in beautiful shady walks. There we wandered, keeping up a running fire of exclamations at the beautiful broken views, gathering now a wild flower, now a fern, or stretching up for a leaf from the masses of thick foliage on the trees overhead. How the hours shot by! Atop of the hill again, we found our way into a castle, in close neighborhood to the cathedral, a charming old piece of antiquity, with its stores of rare, old curious things. I could fill a quire of old-fashioned letter paper and not do half justice to it. So I shan't say anything more about it, but shut both eyes and mouth and get away from Durham, already grown fascinating enough to make me wish I could live in the shadow of that ancient pile with its "gothic shade."

Our route hither lay for the most part of the way along the coast of the German ocean. The white breakers burst right beneath us sometimes, sending their roar to our ears. Away off occasionally glimmered a dream-like sail, or a phantom stretch of smoke from some passing-out-of-our-world vessel. Near enough for a good view we saw,

"Markworth, proud of Percy's name,"

very literally a "castle by the sea," as it seemed as if washed by its waves. The country landward was prettily rolling and laid off in fields of grain and pasture. Great flocks of sheep speckled the latter. A Scotch lady got into our "compartment" when we were still some miles from "Dun Edin." She was very companionable and pointed out all the features of note as they came in sight.

The sun as it went down was a great puzzle to us; it seemed to be setting in the east, and we could not get it to fit the points of the compass stowed away in our craniums. You see it did not set till nearer nine than eight o'clock, and that gave it time to get almost round to where it had started from! The Scotch welcome quite won our hearts. We had written and engaged rooms a week before, so knew we would be expected. The landlady and three daintily-arrayed maids were in the hall, and the former, Mrs. Campbell, stepped forward and took our hands, with the sweetest-voiced welcome! We felt at home at once. Just here I think I must give you a list of the people collected under her roof—tourists, here for a day or weeks, as may chance: an Episcopal High Church curate, from Wales; a Mrs. Smith and her daughter, from Australia; a Mr. Bruce, from the Cape of Good Hope (he was there when Stanley went there with the remnant of the host that made the trip with him "Across the Dark Continent"); a Mr. Masters and wife, from another part of South Africa, he an emigrant from Yorkshire and she a native born, but the daughter of an emigrant; a lady who resides in Oxford and is enthusiastic about it as a place of residence; two young ladies from the south of England; another two, sisters, from London;

a Miss Gurley, a Scotch maiden lady, a great traveler and linguist, and altogether charming. She had been to the United States and Canada, three times. While in the United States, she was the guest of Bishop Potter. She belongs to Edinburgh, is living across the Firth, among the hills of Fife, not far from royal Falkland. Add us three Americans, and I think it could be called a mixed household, indeed.

L. G. C.

Edinburgh, July 4, 1882.

EDINBURGH.

WE spend our days as usual, "sightseeing." The first place we sought was Holyrood Palace. It is not palatial compared to Windsor, Hampton Court, and the situation is not a cheerful one—low, in a kind of a hollow. I can imagine it oppressively gloomy to a young girl of nineteen, just from gay and sunny Paris, and one of the ornaments of its brilliant court. In the picture gallery there is a lovely, full-length portrait of Mary; but there is a still lovelier picture of her at the castle. I saw her apartments, her bed with its faded velvet hangings, that are slowly dropping to pieces too; one of her paintings on marble, much chipped and defaced, showing no little merit; a piece of her embroidery in a glass case; the little mirror hung on the wall she doubtless took much pleasure in seeing her fair face in; the small supper-room, with its closet, where the dreadful murder of Rizzio was begun, and the splotch of blood on the landing at the head of the stairs, where it was finished. How well we seem to know all about her—

Mary Queen of Scots, Edinburgh.

poor queen, unfortunate and to be pitied, even if as wicked as her worst enemies think. At the castle, on the hill that springs up in the very heart of the city, another suite of "Queen Mary's apartments" is shown, in one of which her son was born. The situation of the castle is incomparably fine. It overlooks the entire city and a wide and varied range beyond. Ben Lomond and Ben Ledi show themselves to the north-west, and on a fair day the Pentland hills lie low and purple in another direction; the Firth carries the gaze with it to the sea in the east, and it is dotted with pretty islands, and its thither side is bounded by the misty shores of Fife. This same view is commanded by Arthur's Seat and Calton Hill. Arthur's Seat is the highest point—everybody and every guide-book says so, and I know it from *experience*, having climbed its 823 feet. We make all kinds of excursions in the environs, and find it the easiest thing in the world to keep up our ecstasies.

Alexander Swift says, "Every true Scotsman thinks Edinburgh the most picturesque city in the world." No wonder. It certainly possesses every feature requisite to constitute that preeminence—"hill, crag, castle, rock, blue stretch of sea, the picturesque ridge of the old town, the squares and terraces of the new"—the quaint streets with their ancient houses "peaked and jagged by gable and roof, and windowed from basement to cope" with those small diamond-paned sashes that seem meant only "to make darkness visible," and yet other streets of a later and more stately architecture; the Nor' Lock converted into a dreamland of park and gardens; the splendid monuments arresting the eye in every direction to recall the illustrious dead and give proof of the appreciation and taste of the living; the hills, crags and slopes that "stand dressed in living green," and the squares and terraces a mass of verdure and flowers—all these and more are the charms of this "Edina, Scotia's darling." Add to them the innumerable resorts, historic, beautiful, grand!—Oh! everything—all around in every direction, and one's sympathy leaps forth to meet that of "every Scotsman."

Now, shall I tell you what a "Bohemian" I have grown to be? Perhaps you will be shocked, but really it is the most fascinating life conceivable, and not to be condemned untried. We go where, and when, and *how* we please; *en grandes dames,* in the conventional splendor of full dress and the swellest turnout of the stand, this always "under protest." Oftener, we set our own "locomotives" to the way and find unsuspected Edens. But oftenest and to my heart's delight, we mount to a super-royal perch *atop of the "tram,"* as the street car is called here, and "view the landscape o'er" at such advantage as no crown or throne can command. And that's the way we went to Morning Side, Edinburgh's Clifton, and to Portobello, its sea-bathing resort. Don't be alarmed though; we are not setting a fashion, only following one already established. If only this mode of traveling were practicable for everywhere. Alas! instead the railway comes in to sadly curtail the enchantment of "views." We had to submit to it in order to see Roslyn Chapel, that ideal morceau of architecture, that exquisite efflorescence of solid rock, that chapel of chapels, "one among ten thousand and altogether lovely." First we struck through Hawthorden, a walk of three miles, beginning with an ordinary park that quickly led to an ivy-mantled ruin, hung on the very brink of a beetling crag, the rock-ribbed foundation of which dropped almost sheer to a swift and clamorous stream two or three hundred feet below. In this underlying basement of rock, queer caverns had been hewn, but farther back than dates reach. We explored them notwithstanding some hesitation, which, however, gave way to the liveliest enthusiasm. In one we came across a sword of Robert Bruce in an open wire case. The meshes were about an inch in length; by counting them I found the sword measured fifty-eight inches. I wondered how much taller the warrior was than his weapon of warfare! Leaving these caverns we were soon descending a path that brought us to the edge of the stream and then ran along it the rest of the way. Anything wilder or more beautiful is rarely met, but I have seen Trenton Falls in my own native land, and it surpasses. Climbing the hill again at the end of the three miles we reached the chapel. Another day we spent at Dunfermline. In the Abbey we stood on the grave of Robert Bruce; it is right under the pulpit. In the ancient and long-disused, but well-preserved, nave we saw that inexplicable caprice or trick of architecture, one of the great Norman columns that scanned from one place shows the upper half much smaller than the lower; from another, the reverse effect, and from yet another, a pillar of perfect proportion. The ruins of the old palace and part of the abbey are very touching and beautiful. It too has "a den," as every deep wooded and rocky glen with a stream running through its dark length is called. We sat on the rustic seat under a grand old tree and looked at the ruins and moralized, raved over the vistas, shadows, flashing sunlight and—munched our lunch. Saturday we skimmed away on the wings of the delicious morning as well as the wings of steam to Dalkeith and Newbattle Abbey to spend the day between the two. The former is the favorite seat of the Duke of Buccleugh, the latter that of his son-in-law, the Marquis of Lothian. The ducal palace is positively ugly; but it has its complement of grand state apartments filled with fine pictures and the usual quota of superb articles of vertu and bric-a-brac.

Newbattle Abbey is a charming *home*. Its park boasts some rare old trees, among them a giant beech that is "a monarch of the forest" verily, measuring twenty-three feet in girth. Thursday we start on our excursion to the Highlands; it will take a week. We shall return here for a fresh departure. Then look out for another half quire of this moving matter.

L. G. C.

Edinburgh, July 21, 1882.

HEIDELBERG.

IN Heidelberg. Think of it! What an energetic idler I am grown! The Neckar lies a pistol-shot from my windows; high hills rise on the thither side, looking so home-like—Maysville home, like Mr. W.'s, where you came once upon a time. When my glance darts out the windows and rests upon them, suddenly I catch my breath, and I am not sure whether it is pain or pleasure I feel. Half way up they are cultivated, but the tops are wooded. Just over my head the old castle looms up among the trees. "The Gardens" of this pension where I am lead right up to it. I shall climb to it to-morrow for the first time. Reached here day before yesterday, late; got settled yesterday for a good rest; shall stay here till the latest season for Switzerland; then it and on to Munich for another rest.

Here's "a mere mention" of where I have been since I wrote from "Edina, Scotia's darling." From there to the English lakes we saw ten each lovelier than the last. I wish you

Pension and Garden to which Goethe wrote a Poem, Heidelberg.

HEIDELBERG. 39

were within sound; how I would *rave* to you! Then ruins. Furness Abbey and Fountain's Abbey, both beyond Melrose, and Dryburg in some respects. London for a week (where we parted). Then to Rochester for its cathedral, castle (a ruin) and Gad's Hill, Canterbury. Oh! Oh! Oh!

Dover, Ostend, "The Belfry of Bruges," Ghent, Brussels, seeing the king and queen gratis, Antwerp, The Hague, Rotterdam (the loveliest and liveliest of them all), Amsterdam, Cologne, Bonn, and a pilgrimage to the graves of Niebuhr and Bunsen, Coblenz, Mayence—from Bonn to Mayence being the grand Rhine trip. "The castled crag of Drachenfels," and innumerable other castled crags, sometimes as many as three in sight; the Lurlieberg; the sweet, song-famous Bingen; the world-wide known wine district, Rheingau, whence come the costliest wines in the world—Johannisberger, Reiderheimer, Steinberger, etc. I saw the Schloss Johannisbergers crowning a lovely vine-clad knoll, the entire vineyard or vineyards comprised in forty acres. The Schloss is a very extensive chateau, but ugly; belongs to Prince Richard Metternich, and yields a neat little income of £8,000 ($40,000). Some of our tobacco acres do almost as well! We climbed the precipitous rock on which "the majestic fortress of Ehrenbrietstein" is situated. It is opposite Coblenz, and we crossed the Rhine to reach it on a bridge of boats. I saw three bridges of this kind. I guess they have been handed down since Caesar's time. I could not find out their special merit. They are not particularly striking—just a number of boats, sharp at both ends, side by side, with the solid flooring and railing of any bridge.

The view from the fortress is one of the finest on this glorious stretch of seventy miles, and I was glad to see it.

I wish I could lend you my eyes for a few minutes, so you could see what I saw. You'd come over and see it all, if it cost you that farm you spoke of in one of your letters, or another book!

L. G. C.

Heidelberg, August 15, 1882.

HEIDELBERG.

I AM just home, this is "home" for the present, from a week's delight at Nuremberg. "Delight," how feeble that sounds. Enchantment, fascination, the absorption that makes one lovingly linger and loth to come away. It is the quaintest, most charming old city, I verily believe, that the sun shines on. From its streets, sometimes wider, sometimes narrower, but always crookeder, to its curious houses with their high-peaked gables and red-tiled roofs, with regular rows of such funny hooded windows let into them, and the upper stories all cut up into the most lavishly ornate towers, balconies, and sculptures; from its ramparts with towers of various forms at intervals, and its dry moat, thirty-five yards wide and thirty-five feet deep, to the river running through and dividing the town into nearly equal parts, spanned by old and historic bridges; from the churches, museums and galleries filled with the masterpieces of Durer, Kraft, Stoss and Vischer, to the shops with their bewildering medley of carvings in wood and ivory, and castings in terra-cotta, bronze and brass, by the thousand nameless artists of to-day; from—oh! everything to everything. Just leave all the rest of Europe out if you can't get it and Nuremberg in. Think how you'd feel to see a lime tree planted by Queen Kunigunde in the year 1002! or a lamp that has never been allowed to go out since it was first lighted in 1326! or a wedding in the Rathhaus! I saw them all. And saw besides, the Crown Princess and her daughter, and was not struck blind by the sight! And there was a great exposition in progress, and yesterday the anniversary celebration of the victory at Sedan. The exposition was a grand and most artistic spectacle; and all "United Germany" a spectacular display of multitudinous flags, and processions enlivened with human huzzas and band music! I wish I dare tell you the half I saw, or a tithe of the ravishment of mind and soul wrought by that picturesque, haunting, old ancestral city of mine. My great grandfather went to America from it. Did I ever tell you? Do you wonder I could not bear to tear myself away? I am going back some day if I have the ghost of a chance.

To-day I have been resting; too tired for church, for anything but this careless scamper over a sheet of paper. Had an interruption in a call from some Cape Colony English ladies, tourists as we are, whom we met at Inverness and went with to the battle-field of Culloden; and again at Dunkeld. My traveling companion, Miss S—— of Boston, struck them quite unexpectedly again yesterday on the "Old Bridge" that crosses the Neckar, which I think I called Maine in my last to you. They are very agreeable, and their party consists of the mother and five daughters. Well, I do think the sheets of paper of the present day have the most limited capacity. I am not half begun and this is used up! Pshaw!

L. G. C.

Heidelberg, September 3, 1882.

BADEN-BADEN.

AS a reward for your reformation I write to you on this precious sheet. You see I have come to be wonderfully attached to Heidelberg, the beautiful, the quaint, the historically poetic, learned and picturesque old town on the Neckar. It seems like another home. So I could not show my appreciation of you in a more complimentary way than by sending this little series of pictures. Have you ever been here, I wonder? You did not say, but you wrote as if you knew it by sight as well as by heart. As I cannot know, I will venture an explanation. The panorama speaks for itself. Put on your "specs" and look at the castle, half way up the *berg*, "the Jettenhuhl, a wooded spur of the Konigestuhl." Look at it from the "Terrasse." Thus you'll get something of an idea of it. The Gesprente Thurm is the one that was blown up by the French. The thickness of the walls, twenty-one feet, and the solid masonry, held it so well that only a fragment, as it were, gave way. It still hangs as if ready to be replaced.

"Das Grosse Fass Gebaude," too, you will have no difficulty in making out. If you only had it with its 49,000 gallons of wine, but wouldn't you divide with your neighbors! The columns in the portico that shows in the Schlosshof are the four brought from Charlemagne's palace at Ingelheim by the Count Palatine Ludwig, some time between 1508–44. The Zum Ritter has nothing to do with the castle, but is an ancient structure (1592) in the Renaissance style, and one of the few that escaped destruction in 1693. It is a beautiful, highly ornamental building, and I wish you could see it, if you have not seen it.

All the above information, I beg you to believe, I do not intend you to think was evolved from my inner consciousness, but gathered from the—nearest guide-book!

I am so much obliged to you for mapping out Switzerland to me. I have been trying my best to get all those "passes" into my brain. Now, thanks to your letter, I have them all in the handiest kind of a bunch. Ariel like, "I'll do my bidding gently," and as surely, if I get there. But there are dreadful reports of floods and roads caved in and bridges swept away and snows and—enough of such exciting items as sets one thinking—"to go or not to go?" We are this far on the way. Reached here this afternoon. Have spent the evening sauntering in the gardens, the Conversationhaus, the bazaar, mingling with the throng, listening to the band, and comparing what it is with what it was. It was a gay and curious spectacle, but on the whole had "the banquet-hall deserted" look. The situation is most beautiful. It lies, you know, at the entrance of the Black Forest, among picturesque, thickly-wooded hills, in the valley of the Oos, and extends up the slope of some of the hills. The Oos is a most turbid, turbulent stream; dashes through part of the town with angry, headlong speed. There is an avenue along its bank of oaks, limes and maples, bordered with flower-beds and shrubberies, and adorned with fountains and handsome villas. We shall devote to-morrow to seeing all there is to be seen, and go to Strassburg to-morrow evening for two or three days. From there to Constance, and then hold *our* "Council" as to further movements.

L. G. C.

Baden-Baden, September 19, 1882.

FROM HEIDELBERG TO NUREMBERG.

JUST after I last wrote I left my companions to worry along over their "German lessons," and ran away to Nuremberg. A very pleasant party was going there on the way to Vienna, and wished me to go along. Of all Germany, divided or united, Nuremberg was my objective point; for in addition to its special attraction as "the most perfect surviving specimen of mediaeval architecture in Europe," it has a nearer interest to me in that it was the home of my father's paternal ancestors, as far back as 1570. So I went with alacrity. We left Heidelberg at the reasonable hour of 10:50 a. m. Thanks to the moderate form of tourist life I have adopted, neither the hours of my "beauty sleep" nor that last supreme "forty winks" of the luxuriant morning sleeper, are ever interfered with. Our way lay up the Neckar, and as the train left the Carlsthor it glided—literally glided, the rate of speed not exceeding from twelve to fifteen miles an hour, and it "the fast train," too! —along the bank of the river, under an avenue of trees, giving ample time for one to take in views that one might delight to shut her eyes and recall in the dreamland hours of some future paradise. There were cone-shaped, beautiful, castle-capped mountains, the long winding valley with the river showing in many a lovely curve and shoot; village after village, in the mellowest tints of Indian red, brown, and drab, gathered around its church or chapel, almost every one with an amazing tall spire; ranges of wooded hills that came together in one direction, or retreated from each other in another, disclosing wonderful vistas;—and the weather! One moment a burst of sunlight; the next a veil of fleecy white clouds that changed into the mistiest blue; presently a dash of rain; then the brilliant clearing up again. Thus continued both views and weather to Heilbronn, forty-two miles. There are two historic points, Wimpfen am Berg, which occupies an old Roman station destroyed by the Huns under Attila; and Sinzheim, where Turenne gained a victory in 1674. I own their history was not half so interesting to me as their beauty. From Heilbronn to Nuremberg, over a hundred miles, the country was one great stretch of farming land, fine soil, and admirably cultivated.

HEIDELBERG TO NUREMBERG. 49

We ran into Nuremberg in a pelting rain. All the hotels full. After being turned away from five, with the most proper apologies be it said, we found lodging, but "no rations" except breakfast, at a private house. This was duly served: coffee, rolls, butter and eggs, the last *raw!* Fancy our amusement. Having left our names at the various hotels for the first vacancy, next morning the Golden Eagle found a place for us beneath its sheltering wings. We were fortunate in the time of our visit—a grand exposition was in progress. Nearly all of "united Germany," as well as "little Bavaria," seemed thronging the hotels and crowding the streets. The Crown Prince and his family occupied two hotels. The exposition continues, and is really a superb attraction. As for the quaint, picturesque old city itself, I cannot believe there is another so fascinating. From its streets, sometimes wide, oftener narrow, always crooked; its houses, eight and ten stories high, with their lofty-peaked gables and red-tiled roofs, with five or more tiers of the funniest little windows; its churches, monuments, and repositories of the best productions of that brilliant constellation of workers—Durer, Kraft, Vischer, Stoss and Hirschvogel—who lived and flourished there together; its shops, tempting with pictures, carvings, castings, and—toys; its museums, that it would take days to tell you about; its curious old bridges spanning the river Pegnitz, that divides it into two parts; the fortifications, consisting of a rampart running round the entire old city, with towers at intervals, and a dry moat, thirty-five feet deep and as many yards wide; its old berg, or castle, that rises on a lofty sandstone rock with "the wide extended prospect" from its walls and windows, and the old lime tree in the court, planted by Queen Kunigunde somewhere from 1004 to 1024; to the cemetery where Durer is buried, with its singular, but the most impressive monuments, plain, massive, low monoliths, with large plates inserted in the tops bearing the inscriptions. From first to last, everywhere and everything, the old town, all alive with the quickest beating of the pulse of the nineteenth century, was a delight and wonder.

Do not dream of a half description of anything; there was too much for one pen—too much for a thousand pens. But you never saw lions, life size, made out of soap, did you? Or temples, pagodas, monuments of every design, made out of buttons, matches, tacks, not mere toys, but big enough for out doors?

Among others of these artistic and architectural structures, was a tall shaft monument of tobacco, fine-cut, twist, stem, and leaves, labeled—fancy my heart-throb on reading—"Maryland," "Virginia," "Kentucky." And these are some of the innumerable sights I saw at the exposition. What else did I see?

> "Pussy-cat, Pussy-cat, where have you been?
> I have been to London to see the Queen."

I saw the crown princess and her daughter! I looked at them and they looked at me—took me in as they did the shop-windows, trees, whatever came within the sweep of their roving glance—just as I did them! Such a plain, insignificant little party as they were! The crown prince was not with them. Just two ordinary open carriages, the princess in the first, with her daughter by her side; in the other, a lady and gentleman in attendance. They came out from a shop of carvings just as we were approaching it to enter. And I saw a wedding at the chapel of the Rathhaus (town hall)! Neither the bride nor groom was on the sunny side of forty. She was dressed in a rich heavy black silk, with a white illusion head-dress, that was voluminous enough for a veil, though evidently not intended for one. The ceremony was apparently a simple civil service, conducted by the magistrate, or whatever he was, and an assistant. The bridal party was accompanied by one person only—a gray-haired old gentleman.

How the days sped by! The first thing I knew, ere I was half ready to leave, my last day had come. I bought a package of Nuremberg's famous gingerbread, and bidding my pleasant party "good-bye," most reluctantly betook myself to my home-bound train. Traveling, as I was, alone, I was put in the special "ladies'" car, "Fuer Damen," as it is labeled. Presently, another "lone female" was put in, who proved to be a young German lady. I began to stumble in German to her. She smiled, and replied in tolerable English, it being one of the five languages of which she was in a manner mistress; and she was just beginning the sixth! "I have so much time," she said simply, in explanation of such learning. She was educated in Geneva. If she is an average example of its pupils, Geneva's schools must be indeed desirable. And the next thing I knew, our five weeks at Heidelberg were gone, and it was time to "move on" again.

We started for Munich via Baden-Baden, Strassburg and Switzerland—an attractive programme, but not less did it hurt to say another "good-bye" to the pleasant friends we had made—the beautiful Pension, which had come to have a real home feeling; the romantic "ancient university town," and the grand old castle, both Longfellow-haunted to me; and to the various charming places in the environs—become almost as familiar as the favorite haunts of childhood. Our bright little Fraulein, whose dainty motions made one think of a bird's, said in her very best English: "You must tired once more get, and soon again come home." Her eyes were brimming with tears. The good frau mother took me in her arms, and in German fashion pressed each of my cheeks against each of hers. It was a most charming family.

We spent a night at Baden, the great Spa—the ex-gambling hell—the beautiful city that has risen from its degradation and put on robes of innocence. This is due to the efforts of the present and the preceding grand duke, both men of exceptionally noble characters, and warmly honored and loved. The former prosperity and popularity given by the seductions of the gambling bank have been succeeded and surpassed by attractions of a different and higher kind. Instead of the dreadful fascinations of the Cursall, the palatial Friedrichsbad, said to be the most complete bathing establishment in the world, offers the healing and luxury of its thermal and mineral baths. It takes its name from the reigning grand duke, who was its chief and most intensely interested projector. But his wise exertions and princely tastes have apparently known no restrictions. They have been shown in the erection of other magnificent buildings, in the laying out and exquisite adornment of public parks and promenades; indeed in doing everything possible to render Baden not only a delightful summer resort, but suitable for a permanent home.

It is provided with theaters, balls, fine music, scientific lectures, etc. The results justify his efforts and sagacious foresight. Wealthy families of rank all over Germany are making it a home. Do I seem to dwell on Baden and its grand duke? Well, I may as well admit, all the homage I am capable of is evoked by such a man and such a work. I have his photograph and many little pictures of his Baden! Have you ever read in a way that impressed you to remembrance of the beautiful situation of Baden? The highest compliment that can be bestowed, as the guide-book says, is this: "It vies with Hiedelberg."

It lies among picturesque wooded hills, at the entrance of the Black Forest, on the Oehlbach; it is on the right bank of the stream, and runs up "a slope of the Battert," the summit of which is crowned by the New Schloss, one of the grand duke's residences. It has a Saratoga look. Have n't all watering places a close kin look? But it has its own foreign look too, and distinctive features, even from those of Weisbaden, its rival.

On the left bank of the Oos—"the well corrected Oos," as I have seen it called somewhere, because it has been confined for some distance between high stone walls—are the pleasure grounds, the Conversationhaus (the old Cursaal), the Trinkhalle on one side of an open square, full of avenues of shade trees, and in one corner of which is the gay and fanciful "Music-Kiosk," where the band plays, and the Lichtenthale Allee. This last is an avenue of "vanishing distances," of lime trees, oaks, maples, flowerbeds, shrubberies, fountains, and all kinds of ornamental seats scattered through it. The Oos, the most turbid, turbulent strip of a river, dashes along as if in a perfect fury at those confining walls. The walls themselves, though, are a special feature of the rare loveliness that meets the glance on every side; they are so festooned and draped with vines one can scarce more than guess at the stones so veiled. The Virginia creeper was so in excess the river seemed rushing between a running fire of crimson flames. It was indeed "exceeding beautiful." In the evening we walked in the brilliantly lighted square, peering into the gay shop windows, stopping to listen to the band, mingling with the throngs of well-dressed people, and bringing up in the "great saloon" (fifty-four yards long and seventeen wide) of the Conversationhaus for a rest and a study of the novel scene. Finally we strolled through the two old gambling saloons (the Landscape and the Italian) and ever so many others, and lost ourselves in admiration of the beauty and comfort. The next day we spent in driving to the Old Schloss, six miles from town, on a high "berg," and to all the points of most interest. The Old Schloss is a very romantic old ruin, and commands the finest views around Baden. From it we went to the New Schloss, and were shown through a number of handsome saloons and the apartment of the grand duke and duchess. It was such a perfect little gem of an apartment that I must give you a peep into it. A comparatively quite small oblong room, with two doors opposite each other and in the middle of each wall. One end of the oblong was a dead wall, the other a large bay window of the loveliest stained glass, in pictures of all the choicest points about Baden. Only the center pane was plain glass; it too, though, framing a lovely view of the scene outside. The doors were rather doorways, being, I should think, ten feet high by four wide, all apparently one solid magnificent mirror. As one steps across the threshold, himself or herself is beheld before, behind, on either hand, overhead, in infinite repetition. The French custodian made merry in showing off this ingenious and amusing trick of reflecting surfaces. After this came the Friedrichsbad, with its innumerable varieties of baths, the Trinkhalle and a glass of its steaming water, and—"and other things too numerous to make mention of," to quote from our old town crier.

With decided reluctance we set our faces toward Strassburg, where, to be sure, we wished to go, but we did not feel ready to leave Baden.

We spent two days at Strassburg. You know there was the grand Cathedral, with its grander clock, to see, the fortifications, some fine public parks, and the immense Alsatian bows with the women attached, besides a lunch on the famous local dish, pates de foie gras. I circumnavigated the Cathedral, loitered through and through it, and finally sat down before the clock at the stroke of eleven, to watch it through the next hour. I saw the little boy come out and strike his quarter and disappear, the youth, the middle-aged man, the old man; and then the grand midday procession of puppets representing the Apostles, pass before another puppet representing Christ, making fitting reverence, all but that dreadful Judas, who turned his back on him. The cock, too, performed beautifully, flapped his wings and stretched out his neck, and crowed a sure-enough chanticleer crow, loud enough and cheerily enough to waken the soundest sleeper and make the laziest willing to creep out of bed. The little angel turned his hour-glass, the show was over, and I came away very much impressed with that wonder of mechanism which has been running and regulating itself ever since 1842, and is calculated to do this for an unlimited number of years. And don't you think I did right to shut my ears and refuse to listen to a young Yankee "Paul Pry," recently from a six months' sojourn in Strassburg, who wished to make me believe there was a man behind performing a la—the organ-grinder! The Alsatian bows were a perpetual feast of fun, but as a feast of the palate once is often enough for me of the pates de foie gras.

From Strassburg through the Black Forest by rail was a run of 728 miles. We had a series of thirty-eight tunnels in succession. The very foundation rocks of the earth seem to have been blasted and dug through to make this admirable road; the round charms of which could not be summed up in a Summer day's gossip.

L. G. C.

Munich, September 27, 1882.

LETTER FROM MUNICH.

BADEN was perfect in its way, and we left reluctantly. We "did" it quite thoroughly—had a six mile drive to the Old Schloss, a fine old ruin, on top of a high hill, with beautiful views of bergs, valleys, and the town.

Then a visit to the New Schloss, one of the residences of the Grand Duke. We were shown through some noble apartments, which I'll describe to you in detail when we meet. We went to the Trinkhalle and drank some of the streaming water. The others made faces, but I did not find it unpleasant. Then through the great Friedrichsbad, the principal bath-house. I believe it furnishes every kind known to science or desired by either suffering or luxurious humanity. And so on. At Strassburg, the Cathedral with that wonderful clock! "The half has not been told," and it does not begin to come up to the reality. The way that cock flaps its wings, stretches its neck and crows is enough to make all created cocks die of envy. At St. Thomas Church, with its magnificent monument to Marshal Saxe; and its most singular chapel, con-

MUNICH.

taining the bodies of the Duke of Nassau and his daughter—the former embalmed, the latter a slowly crumbling skeleton—both dressed in the very clothes they wore! I cannot imagine a more ghastly and singular spectacle than that of each lying there in an air-tight coffin, the entire top of glass, thus allowing a full view.* Yet it was not revolting to me, except as the dead were made a spectacle of. I gazed at them with an equal fascination and reverence. We were much interested in the fortifications, great numbers of soldiers and their drilling.

And we did not fail to indulge in the Strassburg specialty of pates de foie gras. I was reminded of a criticism on a juvenile composition of mine by one who knew how *not* to withhold the wholesome truth: "Its individuality is not sufficiently palpable." At Constance we held our "Council," and the reports from Switzerland being very unfavorable, decided to put it off to a more auspicious season.

Constance is a most charmingly situated and attractive little city. We stayed at the Insel

---

* My memory is in a fog, but I think it was beneath this monument I had just read these words of comment: "Baedeker says the old gent"—when I was ruthlessly hurried away; and now I shall never know what Baedeker said. All the same, I feel sure Young America was the irreverent commentor.

Hotel, the old monastery, in which Huss was imprisoned, you know; and I saw the cell in which he was confined. It was underground, and its walls were washed by the waters of the lake. I set my feet on that white spot in the slab of the nave of the Cathedral where he stood when he was condemned to be burned at the stake. You remember it is said to remain dry always, even when the rest is wet. Finally, we drove to the stone that marks the place where he and Jerome suffered that dreadful sentence. It is a pile of rocks, all overgrown with ivy and other vines, except where slabs show through bearing commemorative inscriptions.

From Constance to Lindau we had an enchanting sail over an emerald sea, with many a pretty village gleaming along its shore, "like a white swan on her reedy nest;" and then green hills, that soon turned into denser clouds, as it were, and directly, almost in a flash, the snow-covered Alps!

Railway from Lindau here; and such a succession of pictures! Long, green valleys, dotted with picturesque villages; chains of wooded knolls; ranges of dark, pine-covered mountains, overtopped in places with a vast jumble of cones; snow-covered Alps again, that shone in the sunlight like molten silver! Words avail little toward reproducing such a panorama. Only one's own eyes can do it even the faintest justice. I hope you have seen it, or, if not, will some day *soon,* before you grow an old man. Have had a long, lazy, inconsequential, just-going-anywhere-I-pleased stroll this perfect afternoon. The sky is without a fleck; the air crystal clear; the sunshine just that happy mingling of warmth and bracing quality that makes mere animal existence an ecstasy. I could have walked to the uttermost ends of the earth in it. The streets are wide, clean, admirably paved, handsomely built; fine houses of beautiful designs in a soft, creamy-white stone. Parks, gardens, avenues, open squares, trees, flowers, grass, and grand monuments are innumerable. I felt as if I were under a spell of enchantment. What a place to shrink from was "indoors!" I stayed out till the very last moment.

What a city indeed is this Munchen, the capital of "pretentious little Bavaria!" Think of the days of delight before me in its vast halls of art! I am sure you will, and with an added invocation out of your kind heart for whatever else may be good for me.   L. G. C.

Munich, September 24, 1882.

MUNCHEN.

THIS moment finished the second reading of yours of 22d. Ah! there are some things you don't have any conception of; for instance, you don't know how good it is to get a letter from home in a foreign land. I do. Oh! Oh! Oh!

I came in from the opera, Beethoven's "Fidelio," in German, in a "rapt ecstasy," and, in the act of seating myself at our "after the play little supper," I saw your letter lying on my plate. I am intuitive; I knew it was from you. I picked it up and laid it down with the address on the under side. What would "Goggles" say to that? No; he is not a woman; he is not Miss S——. The French have a proverb that runneth in this wise: "La patience c'est la genie." If it had been wisdom those keen little epigrammatists would not have missed it so. However, I do not wish to discourage you in the exercise of that passive virtue; rather let it "work its good and perfect work." Miss S——, not "Goggles," then said: "Why are you not going to read your letter; will it keep?" Of course I blushed and hung down my head and simpered, and—but you've seen the process many a time. Now, what would you give to know how soon I got through with that dainty meal, and hurried away to be "all alone to myself," to pore over the letter that confessed to *two* "love letters" to another woman. It does not need you or anybody else to convince me I am the superarchangelic creature I was reported to you. I know it myself now! See how good I am to write at this late hour, not finding it possible to put you off to that will-o'-the-wisp time, "a more convenient season." And so glad of the love letters; not jealous a bit, because they went where I want them to go! "Don't worry in well doing," "effuse," "flow like the lava," "let all the currents of your being set that way," and so come into possession of that great estate which all the kingdoms of the earth cannot match—"a noble woman nobly planned." Oh, please, I did not write those letters for any one but my sister-in-law. She cut them up, and pieced them together again to suit them to "print." After they were published she wrote what she had done, begging my forgiveness, but making such an appeal in behalf of the paper I not only could not condemn, I even had to tell her she might do as she pleased with my letters to her, *only my name must not be known in connection* with them. You fairly frighten me when you speak of them in the same breath with your friends Mr. W—— and "E. A." Indeed, I feel timid about writing to you, since you have such letters as theirs. Only, we write to each other for the simple "fun of the thing," not giving much heed to anything else, don't we? And, on the whole, I hail from "Old Kaintuck," and that does n't mean cowardice in any direction exactly!

I wish you could have been with me in Nuremberg—my heart city. You'd have seen things too—all that I did not see; and between us there would not have been much left behind. I am going back there some day—ah! that misty future—it may be as the children are credited with saying, though I never heard them, "before soon," and it may be when I die and am resurrected there. This Bavarian soil has a curiously homey tread. I can easily see how I might linger here, "maybe for years, maybe forever." So much to do; so many places to go to; so much to see; such food for thought, imagination, for *dolce far niente*. You know the kind of pabulum that witching state of existence claims, but who can describe it? I am tempted to give you "a sample day" out of this wonder life in Munich. Do I count egotistically when I admit I count on your caring for it, because I *count on the interest of friendship?* Did I tell you to expect and excuse repetitions? Think how many letters I write, and every one wishes to hear everything, and I try not to disappoint.

We are fortunate in pensions. I am on Maximilian Platz, and my windows look out on, first, the Schiller Monument Platz, an exquisite memorial platz, all to itself; a semicircle, with a thick half belt of trees for the background; in front an oval plat of grass, bordered with a bed of flowers, in the center of which stands the statue in bronze on a white marble pedestal. Just in front of it, grown in the grass, is an evergreen wreath; beyond it rise, above a thicket of trees in their rich Autumn tints, the towers of the Wittelsbach Palace, the residence of Ludwig (grandfather of the present king) after his abdication, Brienner strasse on one side and Maximilian Platz (a great semicircular street) on the other. By the way, they converge, the latter here running into the other, and thus making an end of itself, from a spacious boulevard and driveway, around which are blocks of fine edifices in a cream-colored stone. Immediately beneath my windows is a small triangular platz, a *bijou* of a beer garden, in trees and vines, a gorgeous mosaic of greens, golds, browns and scarlets, and bowers and tables, and chairs and shaded lamps, the kind that make moonlight.

Well, I begin the day with my breakfast in my own apartment, all alone. That's the custom of the country, you know, not my indolence. With that spectacle to interest and claim my eager eyes, I shall give you day before yesterday. At 10 a. m. Miss S—— and I went to the palace, which means an entire square composed of three immense palaces—the Konigsbau, the Alte Residenz, or Old Palace, and the Festsaalbau—each occupying one side of the square; the fourth being filled up with the Court Chapel and Court Theater. The greater part of all these is accessible, which makes so much to be seen it has to be taken in "broken doses," *so zu sagen*. The Schatzkammer (Treasury) was our objective point. We ran the gauntlet of soldiers on guard, a spacious court with a handsome fountain, a kind of cloistered stretch with a wonderful grotto of shells, a maze of small ante-rooms, till finally, in a state of perfect bewilderment, we were taken in hand by the major-domo, who procured our tickets (a little ceremony requiring your cards and a silver mark), and ushered us into—oh! Monte Christo, the Arabian Nights, that stately pleasure dome that Kublai-Khan decreed in Zanadu! We wandered through them all. First, through a long gallery called the Stammbaum (Genealogical Tree), containing the portraits of the princes and princesses of the house of Wittelsbach. The room itself is most attractive in gold, gilt and white ornamentation, what space is left from the pictures—a collection that any family might be proud of. At the end, "Open Sesame," and a great door flies back, and we enter. I wish I had Ovid's pen, with which he wrote the description of the Palace of the Sun! Such a blaze of diamonds and rubies, and pearls and emeralds, and all the gems of the earth! There was the *Hausdiamant,* a monster brilliant "in the Order of the Golden Fleece;" and the Palatinate pearl, half black, half white; strings of buttons by the yard of diamonds, a central one as large as a silver quarter, encircled by smaller ones; breast-plates, as it were, of pear-shaped pearls dangling from a mesh of diamonds;

crowns of diamonds that had a blinding brilliancy; cabinets filled with vessels made from rich stones and inlaid with the most precious stones; a copy of Trajan's Pillar it took the goldsmith twenty years to execute; and more of such royal belongings than I could get into a day's description.

And one thing not put down in the catalogue: As I was standing transfixed by some ornaments in *pink rubies* and diamonds, over my shoulder sounded the tones of a woman's voice in American English. You ought to have heard the suppressed fervor of my exclamation under my breath: "Oh, you blessed American tongue!" I turned to confront a most agreeable countrywoman, just as eager as myself for recognition on that ground alone. I met her again at the opera to-night, and we had another chat. I think her husband is an artist, as they live in Florence, and he told me he had been over here sixteen or seventeen years, and was "longing to get back home." On leaving the palace, Miss S—— came home; but I wasn't half ready for indoors—never am except at meal-times and bed-time! So I wandered around the streets in the sunshine, looking in the shop windows and picking up a picture here and there—among

The Old Kaiser at Historical Window.

them that of the "Vier Konige," as the old Kaiser calls it, himself holding his baby great-grandson with as proud an air as if it was his own first-born son, with his son and grandson on either side. Four living generations in the same picture is indeed a spectacle to be made a note of.

Another picture was that including the empress, crown princess, and the young mother herself holding her little king. It is a picture beaming with both pride and happiness. That must have been one of life's happy moments—one of the few supreme flashes of earthly felicity. And on compulsion—dinner, always in Germany a mid-day meal. I am a true Bohemian now; but I was a housekeeper once, and I don't like to derange the order of a household, so I am always "on time." After dinner, out again by myself, Miss S—— having a German lesson. First, a call at a book-store for a variety of Munich gossip. The proprietor is a handsome young man—cultivated, traveled, of good family—his father being a captain in the army, and a very genial, well-mannered person. I drop in on him quite often. He has been all over the United States, even to Cincinnati. I did not ask him about W——! As I sauntered out—I do everything just as the whim takes me—I thought I'd have a droschke drive, so I hailed one and stepped in. Oh! the earth, air and sky of these Munich days! A whole week of them, too, of that kind that makes one exclaim, "Mere existence is a luxury."

After awhile I dismissed it at the door of the Kaulbach Gallery. It is not a large one, only a large room, as full as it can hold of the sketches and a few pictures of that popular Munich artist. It is on a retired street; a very pretty, tasteful building in a garden. A few, from one to three or four persons at a time, were coming and going the hour and a half I loitered. I am not going to bore you or any one with a catalogue or description of pictures, but one was so beautiful and touching I want you to look at it a moment through the lens of my—pen. A city still in the shadow of the night; gleams of dawn in the east; just floating up into the clear, higher air an angel clasping a little child in its arms, with only the words "Zu Gott;" such a common idea, so simply wrought out, but I could not get away from it.

The sketches were intensely interesting. Some were outlines with pencil or pen; others quite fully worked out, of nearly all his great masterpieces.

The cunning of his good right hand seemed never to have been at a loss. His portrait, painted by himself, stood on an easel, with three fadeless chaplets placed upon it by that loving homage which honors alike those who give and those who receive.

Out again and on again, turning my feet obstinately from the "home stretch." Several squares took me to the "English Garden," founded by Count Rumford, *our* uneuphonious "Mr. Thompson." Acres of greenery in drives, walks, bowers, lakes, streams, etc., right on the edge of the city. Like Kane and the Polar Sea, I stood on the brink but did n't jump in. I did not quite like strolling in its shady depths by myself. I had driven through, and the knowledge which neutralizes temptation might have had as much influence to the abstinence as the discretion. No bringing myself to the self-application of the word cowardice! Besides, there was counter-attraction somewhere within several squares which I had not seen, Ludwigkirche, with its altar painting, "The Last Judgment," the largest oil painting in the world, sixty-three feet high and thirty-nine feet broad.

Did you know that? I didn't till the guide-book told me. You are welcome to my hard-earned information. I wish I had time to say something I want to just "in this connection." Hm! I haven't; I must hurry on. Of course, the painting is a masterpiece of art. Isn't that the conventional expression that slips so "trippingly" from the half-fledged tourist? Among the spirits of the blessed is that of King Ludwig, crowned with laurels, attained presumably after his separation from Lola; also that of Dante, the poet of heaven and hell, in a red garment; and of Fra Angelico, the painter of Paradise, in the Dominican robe. I did not give a close inspection to the *spirits of the other order.* Vesper service was in progress, and I sat and watched the devout at their aves and paternosters, a scene in its way food for rather painful meditation. Such mechanical worship; such slavish superstition! Descending the entrance steps as I left the church, I was struck by their worn appearance. The daily tread of the multitudes of worshipers has left them almost unsafe. Then I lagged along Ludwig Strasse, the fine street entirely originated by that same King Ludwig who had public spirit and energy enough to hide a multitude of faults.

The sun was leaving me so fast I had to turn homeward, which I did as reluctantly as you turn back from some of your long tramps, I suspect. Isn't a Munich day a rather fascinating span of life? I match the above day by day. Do you know what a large city it is—230,000 population? And how grand and clean and comfortable? I am wishing I could transport it to the United States for myself and my elect ones to dwell in! For oh! such bread and butter and coffee as abound! There! the weakness for creature comfort will not be thrust aside!

Don't you want to know what neighbors I have? A banker at the end of this *etage,* a widower with a cherub of a child, and in the next suite of apartments to mine—a baron! Such a splendid-looking man! If he had only come sooner—you know the adage about propinquity—before I had quite lost my heart! I couldn't help it. I was taken "so unawares"—not in the least dreaming what would be the issue—when I could not wrest my gaze from that superb creature in such brilliant array. Don't tell on me! A Prussian officer! His uniform is the acme of taste, gorgeousness and becomingness; his off-duty saunter on the street the ultimatum of grace; his easy, dignified, unconscious bearing the perfection of deportment. He never stares at one. It was the merest accident that our eyes met, and the damage was done. Our glances got tangled in each other, and the more we struggled the more hopeless the knot. His name? You promise not to betray this weakness—but could I be a true American woman and come abroad and not lose my heart? His name is Legion; for I can't tell them apart any more than I can help adoring them all—the graceful, gracious, gorgeous beings of gold and plumes and cockades and pompons, and altogether *such uniforms!* For what else were they made, indeed? See how I take you into my confidence? And now then, father confessor, having made a clean breast of it, I shall betake myself to my couch, in the words of "Goggles," to "sleep the sleep of youth, innocence and beauty." Did you say you were going to write fortnightly or weekly? The first will be best.

L. G. C.

Munchen, October 23, 1882.

MUNICH.

SAY, how many copies have you of those foaming sheets you sent me from M—— for a letter? And to how many other addresses have they been sent? I am curious to know. They were never evoked by me—of that I am sure. Nor do I attribute their existence to the overwhelming influence of any other special feminine divinity; rather to one of those supreme intervals—his satanic majesty's own—when

"The d—l finds for idle hands
Some mischief still to do."

You were alone; you were "in a state of mind;" you

"Sat in revery and watched
The changing colors of the waves that broke
Upon the idle seashore of the mind."

You summoned up "spirits of that vasty deep, red, white and blue;" the flimsy creatures, what were they but shades of all your divinities, the slim maidens of your boyhood, the stately goddesses of your cavalier period, "the pretty widows" of your "old bachelor" era?" And so with the prodding of that flock of shadows and the impulse of your besetting iniquity you wrote that sample letter—good for one, good for all? I can see the whole performance. Thankee, sir; I am not to be mistaken for one of that throng. There is nothing gregarious about me. Just leave me out when you give your "free lunch" feasts of sauce and sugar-plums! You—

But I enjoyed the composition "all the same." What a pity you have never taken to novel writing. This letter—I can't call it mine, you see, because it belongs to all of them—ah! this letter "shows your hand." Believe me, you've missed your field in literature. Are you too old to begin over? I ask this because I am beginning to have misgivings in the face of my old sturdy belief that one never outgrew the ability to do if only the will were not wanting. I—I—how shall I admit it? I find there are things I can't do. Of course it is because one grows old, even with the best intentions not to. No, I never want to; and here I am minus the roses of other days and plus wrinkles and gray hairs beyond all calculation, and seriously contemplating a mouthful of false teeth. Sigh for me! Was ever anything so lamentable? I am so glad you told me about your evening with my dear friends, the F——s. How plain you made me see the familiar room. It was good of you all to remember me so. They are of earth's choicest—so high-souled, so loyal, so good. I have yet to see the man who does not do homage to Mrs. F——, and the Doctor is one I delight to love and honor. I hope you met my other friend, Mr. W——, of whom I dreamed last night. I was talking to you, and used this expression: "All the wrong he has ever done in his life—all and the only—is to have always done the right." When I awoke I remembered it. How long I have known him—nearly from the beginning—away back yonder when I was a wee thing in pinafores. He said so pleasantly of that long acquaintance: "The first time I saw her she was so high" (meaning the midget I was) "and swinging in an apple tree; and she swung into my heart, and has been swinging there ever since." Are not those the kind of words "for remembrance?" How good he has been to me. Some day I'll make your heart throb, as these human hearts of ours are quick to do, hearing of the great and noble of earth, telling of all he has been to me and done for me in this life of mine, that has been more sorrow and heartache, you know, than comes to many.

If you could know him as I do—I think, no—I know you would appreciate my affection and reverence. His life has been a constant growth, grace overcoming nature, the lower giving way to the higher, conquest upon conquest, till I almost tremble at that nearness to perfection which means fitness for that better Elsewhere, the ultimatum of all our hopes and dreams. Here are words of a man about him: "Isn't his the tenderest, the lovingest, the gentlest, the purest, the whitest and best soul God ever gave to man?" Did ever you know any man speak so of another? Think what mine will be when I give them leave. Do you observe that I speak to you with perfect freedom, having no fear to express my enthusiasm? It is because *I know you* will not transmute the pure gold of such a friendship into any drosser metal. Ah! I shall indeed be disappointed if you do not meet him. You should call on his wife. You would find her very companionable. You remember her that rainy noon call, I am sure.

Dear old M——! It is looking its best for you, is it? Its best cannot be easily surpassed. Those beautiful hills that I seem to have climbed and scrambled over almost as soon as I learned to walk! How it thrilled me to read your words about them! Ah! you cannot know how they look to my eyes, that always see them in a twofold light—that of my vanished past as well as the present! My husband and I were always sweethearts. I do not clearly remember anything farther back than my love for him. He used to bring me the wild flowers that grew all over them; and we have climbed them together many a time and gazed at their beauty together, and planned the future that lay ahead of us in that wonderful sheen and glow that is visible only to such untried and happy beings. Dear hills! beautiful hills! sacred hills! Yes, I know them in their length and breadth, from their high crests almost to their foundation stones. Did you know I was a *grangeress* before we met? Well, I had that kind of possession of them also. From the top of mine, I could stand by a tall, bare trunk—torso, may I say?—of a monarch in its time, and look westward over the range, including Water-works Hill, to Mr. W——'s. I and my dog did it often; sometimes in the dewy mornings; sometimes the sunny noons; sometimes in the long, tranquil slants of the setting sun. Oh! I know those hills, every foot of them, at all hours of the day, in every light, under every shadow, from their oaks and beeches down to their bramble thickets; every wild flower, every noxious weed, petrifactions, pebbles! What have they that is not a part of my very being? Do you wonder I love them?

I wish some one had had a long enough memory to show you where I was born, not because of that unimportant event, but because you can see even now what an exquisite spot it must have been. It is "the point" where Limestone Creek runs into the Ohio. I am always thankful I was born on the banks of a river and in the shadow of the "everlasting hills." We were playfellows, as it were. The shells I have scraped together; the sand hills I have heaped up; the stolen wades in the edge of the water; the skiff rows; the fishing with pin-hooks and worm-bait! Ah! my beautiful river; that you want to spoil to me by crossing against my wish! Is it you who are so "cruel?" If you are still in M——, ask Dr. F—— to show you "the little house where I was born." It was my grandfather's, and my father's is near by. Make some excuse, you two, to get a walk all about them, just to see the views. You will thank me for it, I know.

Why did you not tell me who that "exuberant set" was? Give me the names. There is no curiosity about *me,* you see. As for that counterpart, I don't like to feel there is another so like me. I cannot imagine who she could have been. Next time don't let her escape you. Clutch her with, if need be, that fierce brigand salutation adapted "Your *name* or your life." There has been an annoying individual of that kind here. She even had the exasperating presumption to have not only my initials, but my name. Think of another " Mrs. Laura Collins" roving around Europe, and getting your letters and opening them. Do you think it was any satisfaction to read her indorsement, "opened but not read by Mrs. Laura Collins." The only thing that reconciled me was that she was "Mrs. G. L. C.," instead of "L. G. C." I am glad she has flown "to other parts," and hope we shall not clash again. But wasn't it aggravating? I did not have any mail for two weeks on account of her getting and keeping it. That "Bayerische Vereinsbank," and I let her have "a piece of our mind," I can tell you, about it. Don't be vicious about my "Bavarian officer." That special one I have not seen again, though I "own up" to an eager scanning of every one I meet. To be sure, I have not the least idea I should know him, but I can't keep from looking for him. It was such a peculiar experience, that rencontre. Think of having to lift your eyes to look at one exactly as if in answer to a call, in spite of yourself, and being overcome in the same instant by an utter helplessness to look away, while you became conscious that each was "slowing up in passing," for you know not what might happen next. It was terrifying too, because I am sure he felt as I did, that nothing ought to happen, except that each should keep straight on. We did somehow manage to. But you see I can't keep from telling you everything—after a few rods—I could not help it—I looked after him! not, however, without some feminine craftiness. I made believe I was attracted by a pretty shop window. Oh—h—h—h!

He, too, standing transfixed in the street, was looking back. Then *was* a shock! Then how each hurried away! I plunged into the shop, and quite bewildered the clerk with various wants. I simply did not know what I was asking for. And he! Ah! what has become of him? Alas! I know I shall never see him again! And also, I know equally well—and this is the saddest of it—I should not know him if I did! Could any one be more harmless?

My charming Munich is showing its kinship

to the Alps. The snow is falling fine, thick and fast. I am not quite delighted, because I do not like the "beautiful snow." I meant to have had one whole year of summer time, getting to Italy before cold weather. But Miss B——'s sickness changed my arrangements. The party I joined were to winter here for study. Now it will be January or February before we see that "sunny clime." Still, I am told by those who have been there that February, March and April are *the* months for it. I want to see it only under the most favorable circumstances, so am content to wait. To-night we are to attend a concert of the choicest music, given by some of Germany's finest musicians. We have had two seasons of opera already. I don't know how many more we are to have. Booth is to be here by and by, and *we* mean to give him a welcome indeed! As for chronicling all I am doing, I can't think of wearying you to that extent. But be sure I have no idle days. They are all as full as they can hold. They will do to talk about in that wonderful "by and by" we have laid out in the future. I am sure there are some points in your letter I have not taken up; but I dare not take them up now, lest such length of letter frighten you into breaking off the correspondence. So much valuable time as the reading exacts—how can you spare it? Besides, those points will keep!

I shall expect a full and true and most minute report of your entire visit. Don't keep an item back. It will be ever so mean if you did not write that "next Sunday." Won't you be glad you did, if you did, when you read this? But indeed and indeed, I am very grateful for your letters, and am your friend to my finger tips.

L. G. C.

Munich, November 18, 1882.

MUNICH.

YOUR second Sunday letter just received and read "twice over." You can't realize the pleasure it gives me. No woman is material for a full-blooded Bohemian. Giving myself, as I am trying to do, wholly up to this life, few would believe what a homesick heart is nearly all the time beating beneath my vivacious words —a heart sick for the home broken up forever; for the dear ones that will meet me no more on any threshold this side the grave. Think how I must feel, reading your words about my lost home—how they take me back to it. I shall never see it again. I could not bear it. Yet I am very grateful to you for thinking to tell me about it; the beautiful tree; the kindly intention to send me a leaf; the plan to see it again. May I tell you such thoughtfulness has the tenderness of a woman in it? My mother would have done the same. Thank you for it. And believe me, my heart has never before so accepted you as a friend. It is very gratifying to me to know that you are so delighted with M——. I have always thought it one of the most beautiful, picturesque bits of earth my eyes have ever seen.

Did I not write that Heidelberg, so famous in song and story and guide-books for its scenery, reminds me of it? It is fortunate you are such a walker and climber. No one who is not can know the beauty of this little planet. Be sure to go over all Mr. W——'s hill, or, rather, his chain. I think you will say it is unequaled, or almost so. If you could only have him for a companion, he would show you many points we have enjoyed so many times, morning, noon, and night. There is a moonrise view that would make you speechless with ecstasy. He found it out for the rest of us. One special hillside is full of wild flowers in the later springtime, where in the earlier spring he has a charming little sugar-camp. We have had such frolics and picnics in the sugar-making season! Be sure to find "Maple Point," and the oak tree with the gnarled roots, where we sat to gaze and talk. You can see away across the river there, even to the home of your friends.

We had quite a snowfall on Saturday. Sunday was a day of steady cold. It and to-day were one of the innumerable church feasts—the anniversary of the founding of the order of St.

Elizabeth. You know the story—her great charitableness and her husband's opposition; how he caught her going out with a basket of food and commanded her to uncover it; and lo! when she obeyed, the contents had been changed into flowers—to meet the emergency! Well, the royal family here, the ladies only, belong to this order, and enter into the celebration with great ardor. The first day, the service is a brilliant one, the princesses in fine carriage toilettes, with their gilt and crimson *prie-dieu* and seats, on magnificent rugs, the priests in splendid vestments, the royal usher in blue and silver, and another gorgeous attendant in scarlet and gold. The service is for the *living*. The royal dames give alms. The service to-day was for the dead, with a total change of programme; the church draped in mourning, the princesses and their seats and desks, the priests, and a grand catafalque. This was lighted by innumerable tall wax candles, in tall silver candlesticks. The music was low and solemn; the people subdued and sympathetic. I was much interested in the spectacle. Besides, I had such close and satisfactory views of *royalty!* And, let me tell you, royalty looked at me with quite as much curiosity as I looked at them. One of the princesses is a daughter of the Emperor of Austria. You know the empress is said to be the most beautiful woman on a European throne. She was a Bavarian princess, and her portraits here justify that verdict. This daughter of hers, the wife of a Bavarian prince, cousin to the king, is a tall, elegant-looking creature, one of the most so I have ever seen, with pretty brown eyes, sunny light brown hair and fine complexion. Her mouth and nose spoil her for a beauty. She looks happy and good. The king likes her, and sometimes invites her to dine with him, without including her husband! Don't think there is any scandal; this is simply one of his eccentricities. He *may* be mad, he *is* queer, but his reputation is as spotless as a woman's. Poor king! You know it was a love affair that upset him. You don't know how my sympathies are enlisted in his behalf. And he really seems just to miss being a grand being. The concert was a wild German enthusiasm. The handsome tenor—tenors are always handsome—"nicht war?"—sang twelve songs, so clamorous was the audience; and he looked like—"Goggles," only "Goggles" is even handsomer.

Oh! I have so much to tell you; but yesterday and to-day in the cold, damp church—no

Louis II, the Mad King of Bavaria.

fire or heat even—have given me a dreadful cold, and I must stop and cosset myself and try to get rid of it. Thank you for your liberality about my religion. You are right in your suspicion. Even my good friend Dr. F—— calls me "heterodox." Indeed, I believe my only religion is, that the life be right and then the soul cannot be false.

L. G. C.

Munich, November 20, 1882.

MUNICH.

"YOU couldn't do it again!" I never repeat myself. It would indeed lower my "crest of haught" to find such barrenness or stinginess of entertaining powers as that shows. "Madam, there be those more gifted who make a point of repetition; it is set quite above your contempt," will you say? Do not I know that? I can quote you the prettiest kink in rhyme "o' that side of the question." Listen:

> "That's your wise thrush; he sings his song twice over,
> Lest you should think he never could recapture
> That first, wild, passionate rapture."

And I could show you in the daintiest script where one "not all unknown to fame," a latter-day writer of much popularity, as I have seen stated, raves and raves again over "the sweet widows." Such things stare me in the face and might silence me, so potent is the force of example. But was ever woman made so meek and yet so set in her own way? Even your taunt does not goad me to a second letter of "the altogethery" type. I—I think indeed I only wish to show you

I know the trick of that style without the help of wine or whisky. Pitiable pair, your Byron and Sheridan! Please, sir, you insist upon my style so much, you wonder more and more where I picked it up. I am urged to ask, is it all style and no sense? I am sure I told you once I picked it up where I picked up my brains. I don't see why you do not accept that statement. You will never get nearer the truth, will you?

"True it is, and pity 't is 't is true."

I re-read the passage at once, and it reads just as I wrote you—"in," *not* "within." I reckon you'll have to come down, "Capting Scott;" not I "cushion my claws." But a victory is twice a victory when the victor is generous. I shall not sing peans over your "altogetheriness." "Poetical justice" is divine when it is on the right side of the river.

How you linger in the land of enchantment! Who would not under the same witchery? "The divine weather" and Hood will help us out—

"Oh! there's nothing in life like making love,
Save making hay in fine weather."

It is always violent when the attack comes late in life—like whooping cough, measles, etc. But I'd by all odds rather have it then than not at all. The life that misses that delicious frenzy is a failure. Yes, I see you like the Indian summer. Just a sentence about it from your sympathetic pen, and you make picture days float before inward eyes. The languid, indolent, dreamy lapse of the autumnal sunshine; the ground beneath the walnut trees black with fallen nuts—I can hear them dropping from the branches, and the excited barking of the pretty gray squirrel; "clear, running brooks," their babble somewhat deadened by their "freighted argosies" of dead leaves; flecks of grass here and there, green as that of early summer; misty distances, half blue, half gold; purplish shadows where the sun does not strike; flocks and herds browsing as if they too were more than half dreaming; farm-houses dotting the landscape, with their great orchards near by—oh! the heaps and heaps of "golden pippins," "rosy-cheeked bellflowers," "Rome beauties," "tawny russets," and so on; and the cider-press, with its running stream, and the big bucketfuls carried to the house; and the sheets of "piping hot" gingerbread waiting for them!

Yes, that is what you make me see. And maybe one's sweetheart made it while he was fetching the cider! Be sure they will eat and drink together! Don't you see their eyes foaming over with felicity? Bless me! I shouldn't wonder if you were the very fellow. Napoleon knew all about that sort of bliss: "The happiest hours of my life were those I spent *eating cherries with my little sweetheart* when I was a boy."

Shouldn't wonder if they had a frolic shooting the seeds, should you? *It* used to be a farm, that place "on the Ohio side" you took in with the "Germantown view." Perhaps that's where you got your "Indian Summer of life" taste!

When your gaze went wandering and "lingering lovingly" in that direction, did it light on the two mounds that give their own interest to
"That vale of Aberdeen,
The vale of gold and green?"

There's a distich of Mr. W—'s for you—I hope so. Were you alone? or accompanied by "an exuberant set," I wonder. Surely, either way, some one must have told you of the mounds. Perhaps your "most pretentious" prattler would have told you they were antediluvian as well as anti-historic. It is plain she would have given some astonishing turn to the crank of knowledge. And had your exclamatory friend been present he might have added to the hilarity of the occasion with some such remark as—I have had so many interruptions, that flash of brilliancy has escaped me. Please put it in for me. You can do that, though you begged off on the cat. Yet you knew! You did not fool me a bit with that pretense of worrying all night. In fact, if you only remember that I am on the shady side—almost shaky—of the autumn of life, the "Indian Summer" which you enjoy, you will forbear any attempt in that direction. How gently you put it—"You'll know about it one of these days," just as if I didn't already know. Some "antique gems" are afraid of their antiquity: others are worldly-wise enough to know it is that which gives them their value: while a rare few shine resplendent in that gracious acceptance of the course of nature, which takes captive "Old Father Time," and converts the awful conqueror into the loyalest henchman. I at least feel no shame of my plus half-century of years. Though, maybe, my counter weakness is the hope of growing into one of that "rare few," the beautiful "old ladies" I have known, and loved, and revered, and been made a little friend of when I was young! Their memory is one of my richest treasures. And now that their crown of years is hovering over my own head, may I prove worthy to wear it.

Was n't I right when I said, "all such gravitate to you as apples and cannon-balls to the ground?" I might have said, more simply, as "the sweet widows" gravitate to you, only I did n't think of that in time. It was the happier "afterthought." See how you are attracting all the most felicitous marvels of speech and gossip garnered in the memories of the experienced; now rising to the surface and exploding like bubbles in the froth of talk; now bobbing here and there like cork in the current, as light and imperishable! What store you will have for illustrations in some future "Noctes Ambrosione'!" That singular death-bed speech I heard of by accident. The person was not a friend; I just knew her, though she was connected by marriage with connections of mine in the same way. It seems to me she died years ago, though I do not know. Who was "the clergyman's" wife that told you? Why are all your friends left unnamed? Have n't they been christened yet? It seems the strangest thing that you should have got hold of that speech! The mere fact haunts me. Was Mrs. M—— the divine musician? Front street west of Sutton runs so far—way down around the point, where you'll lose sight of the old city, "with its dozens and dozens of agreeable people." I can't go prying into every house all that way to find out who she was. Please hereafter mention names.

I never read your side-splitting "French book," "Petty Annoyances," but I'll get it to-day if I can. I have read some of that "bad fellow's" books for the French some years ago. Since I have been here I have been reading Souvestre and Sainte-Beuve. I always liked the former. His was a noble soul, and I am sure he never wrote a word that he repented of on that too early death-bed. Did you ever read his "Au Coin du Feu," a collection of stories? It shows his sweet, good, wise spirit. You must have read his "Attic Philosopher." It had a great run, I remember—how many years ago? Sainte-Beuve I feel sure you know. I enjoy his incisiveness and his (on the whole) impartial criticisms. But I am "over head and ears" in Dutch reading: am now deep in the "Nibelungenlied." Having seen the Nibelungenlied suite of rooms in the king's palace, I wished to read the story in the original. I had read it in English "ever so long ago"—long enough for the mists of memory to have made a blur over some of the details. I sat up

MUNICH.

till midnight reading it—couldn't stop, though knowing I should. It cannot need other evidence of its fascination. The frescoes at the palace no doubt added to the interest. They are hauntingly wonderful and beautiful. Even the extraordinary chanting of the story of each by the stolid guide could not spoil the impression. If ever I have a chance, I'll favor you with a specimen of his performance. Alas! that I shall not have the cut and tinsel of his royal livery! How I wish you could see all the treasures of this "king's palaces." They have been gathered from a range of time reaching as far back as his ancestral line, to 1180. I doubt if any other royal line can quite equal it in many things. And the opinion is not held in the interest of my Bavarian blood either.

Now, tell me quick about "the last from B——." Don't keep me waiting. "Dogs and children cannot bear suspense," and I am just like 'em. And when are you going to tell me all about the sweet detaining cause? I am a paragon of a confidante. Try me. I shan't tell it to one, and then she can't tell it to two. And so A. P. R. will have nothing to rue. Impromptu sparkle! Catch it and preserve it under glass.

L. G. C.

Munich, December 12, 1882.

MUNICH.

JUST see what your last letter has done. You wished my "counterfeit presentment." Here it is. Will you be pleased with it, I wonder?

Had you called on Mrs. W——, as you should have done, you'd have seen a life-size crayon copy of "that same," which Mrs. W—— had done in Washington. It is considered a superb picture and a perfect copy, which makes it a matter of inferior moment if it is no particular likeness. It was very well for Cromwell to insist, "Paint me as I am;" but for a woman, if the beauty is there, paint her as she is; if not, paint her as she should be.

The photographs I have rejected, destroyed or hid away from sight forever, because of the lack of this essential! This Munchen artist kept coaxing: "Look brighter;" "smile;" "*don't* look so sad;" "you look as if you had not a friend in the world;" till I tried my best. "There, that is good;" "that will do;" "now"—and he "turned the sun on." All the same, I am not a picture woman, and I know it. "Why, bless you! of course you don't make a good photograph."

"Don't you know why?" said a friend in Philadelphia a few years ago, ere the brown was silver and the roses had faded; "I can tell you." I looked an eager inquiry. "When you sit for a picture your face is discharged of all expression, and the glow of the roses can't be shown in black and white." But wasn't he a comforter!

Yes, the home of my childhood, but not the house in which I was born, is gone. I was born in the large old-fashioned house nearest the mill. I think it is now occupied by a Mr. L——. You must have noticed it. It is a pleasant-looking place even now; spoiled as all the Point is by those later houses. When we lived there the houses of my father and grandfather were the only ones for perhaps a quarter of a mile. There were, maybe, a dozen houses in "Newtown," as it was called then. There was no street except on the river bank in front of our places. The front yards of both were full of grass, plants, flowers and shrubbery. My mother had so many roses, ours was called "The Place of Roses." Each had large gardens and meadows and orchards. Some of the pear trees are living and flourishing now, over a hundred years old!

I thought seriously of buying the place of my grandfather when I sold my other one; went and looked at it several times, but I was too alone to attempt another home. Now I am sure it was best I did not. You can comprehend how it made my heart ache to hear of that fire. I have not been in the house for years; I think not since my father moved into Maysville, and in all probability would never have been again, but the pain is inevitable.

I have found and read "Les Petites Miseres de la vie Conjugale." Psha! Don't you believe him—that ruthless anatomist. I believe I could forgive him if he had not made these "Annoyances" so life-like and comical. I laughed even when I was "boiling over with rage" at his revelations. Wish I was not so indolent; I'd write a counter-statement if I were not! I could, and it would be the God's truth, just as his is the devil's truth. But for one thing I'd set you to do that "spiriting." So unfortunately you lack *experience!* But why could n't you, any way, just as well as "Ike Marvel" wrote "Dream Life?" Did you ever read "the Pendant" to "Les Petites Miseres, Les Menages d'une femme vertuense?" I got it at the same time, and found it intensely interesting as a picture of French character and life. But I must not get on to books, or I shall write all night.

Do you know Christmas is coming? It is so near it takes my breath away to think of it. This is Friday night—and Monday! I'll catch you anyhow, " My Christmas Gift." Isn't that the way you shouted it as you tiptoed round in the early dawn of Christmas morning, when you were a boy? And hadn't you already hung up your little sock the night before, knowing you would find it stuffed full of "goodies and things?" I had a young bachelor friend in C——, "a fellow of infinite jest," and much curious and quaint humor. He was alone at home, so I sent for him to dine with us.

"What did you do last night, John? Were you not lonesome? Why did you not come round?"

"Oh! I read awhile! Then I ate apples and nuts. It was lots of fun to roast the apples and hear them sizzle and sputter and burst, to say nothing of the eating and burnt fingers. And you never saw 'a stoker' (I think that was the word) beat me at keeping up a fire with my nut-shells. When I got tired, I *hung up my sock* and went to bed."

Will you do the like? I hope you will have "the goodies and things," whether you do or not. Yes, I hope you will have the very best Christmas of all your life. It is to be very "gay and festive" here, and I shall see many novel and magnificent sights. Maybe I'll tell you about some of them.

A merry Christmas! A happy Christmas! The best Christmas of all your life!

L. G. C.

Munich, December 22, 1882.

MUNICH.

ALL the world has been at its busiest getting ready for Christmas, and the amount of knitting and embroidery is overwhelming. I pity eyes. Even the blind do the most wonderful knitting. I was at the Blind Asylum not long ago. There were drawers and drawers full of tidies, caps, stockings, drawers, etc. Some of their customs are rather startling just now. Sunday is never very different from other days, except in the church services. The shops are kept open till late in the afternoon. All the world goes to church, and then to the military parade, and to hear the band play in one of the public squares, and then to shop! At home, the afternoons and evenings are spent in fancywork of whatever kind may be on hand, or in games or dancing. The last three weeks, our young ladies have embroidered indefatigably all Sunday, except when at church or shopping. I am sure I don't like this custom; but Christmas is a grand festival in Germany, you know, and I suppose it would be heart-breaking not to make the most ample preparations. The last two days, cooking has been the duty of the frau-mother. She prepares all her cake, but sends to a regular baker to have the baking done. You ought to have seen the display when it came home! They were brought on great table-tops (I don't know what else to call them). On one I counted thirteen immense loaves; on another as many or more. All were nicely iced, or dusted with sugar, and they looked very inviting. The baker says no one sends him such rich batter as our frau—so full of almonds, citron, etc. One of the young ladies made "a whole lot" of almond macaroons. They are delicious. What an experience this, of spending Christmas in a German household! We are having a real homelike Christmas-time. A beautiful tree—all of us were called on to help adorn it. Our presents are not wanting. I received a pocket-handerchief embroidered by the oldest daughter, an apron embroidered by the second, and a beautiful satin glove-box embroidered and made by the third, Gretchen. The mother gave me a copy of the "Neibelungen-lied" in German, and a great waiter of all kinds of "goodies," to be kept in my own apartment. But the best gift of all was the warmheartedness.

Christmas night, I was at the grandest concert I ever attended: Beethoven's Ninth Symphony, and a new thing, "Christoforous," a legend of the Christ-child, arranged in solos, choruses, and for the orchestra. I think it was the first time it has been given here. Jammed house; spell-bound audience; all kinds of people, and toilets to match, from the most superb and fashionable to the very plainest.

It is impossible to live in this wonder city and not find each day adding to one's admiration for its kings. The most ardent republicanism cannot withhold this. Their munificent public spirit, grand conceptions, fine taste, good judgment, energetic execution, and practical improvements are made manifest in every direction. Bavaria, and especially this, its capital city, have been subjected to much criticism and no little ridicule on account of their so-termed pretentious development—their egotism in attempting to rival Athens and Rome in the style and magnitude of their public buildings; their "towering ambition," as displayed in the number and size of their art works; all being regarded as quite out of proportion to its insignificant limits and lack of importance as a political factor in the nations of Europe. But whatever creates business attracts population, adds to the prosperity and increases the revenues of a country; and this is surely no contemptible desideratum in its political economy. That these results have been accomplished here is shown by the census. Bavaria became a kingdom in 1806; Munich is the capital, you know; its population in 1840 was about 40,000; in 1850, 100,000; in 1870, 170,000; the last census, it was over 230,000, and gaining all the time. In every direction, new streets are being laid out, new buildings are going up, old ones are being repaired, and the entire city gives the impression of rapid growth and increasing prosperity, all improvements being of the most substantial and imposing character.

The reigning house of Wittelsbach dates from 1180. It has ruled under the titles, duke, elector, one emperor and king; that of duke till 1623; the one emperor, Elector Charles Albert becoming Emperor Charles VIII from 1726 to 1745. Maximilian Joseph succeeded as elector in 1799, holding that title till 1805, when he was invested with that of king—"Maximilian I, King of Bavaria." The present king is his great-grandson. In otherwise idle hours, I have had the curiosity to make a kind of catalogue of the public work of these rulers. You see, when one is driving or walking in a strange city, the questions are apt to come "in battalions." In my first drive, the finest streets and buildings evoked some such questions and answers as these: "What street is this?" "Ludwig Strasse, planned and built by King Ludwig!" "What building is this?" "The Royal Library, also built by him." And so on till I became quite bewildered by the many magnificent structures and institutions of his creation, or of other kings. But I have continued to question, read, and keep count, till I feel quite familiar with these kingly monuments, and have taken much interest in my "busy idleness."

Maximilian I founded new suburbs: the general hospital which I have visited and inspected closely, and cannot praise too much, a riding school, observatory, and the celebrated bronze foundry, much patronized by the United States. His crowning honor to me is that he was the first German prince who granted a representative government to his people. Ludwig I, his son and successor, began his extraordinary career as patron and lover of art while yet crown prince. His works abound in such numbers, splendor and variety, it is difficult to realize them as the creations of one person, one lifetime. Of course you are familiar with the character of the most, if not all, but perhaps have never "taken the trouble to do this little sum in addition. So I shall only mention the names: the Glyphothek Exhibition Building, Propilae, Old Pinakothek, New Pinakothek, Royal Library, University, Bronze Foundry, Stained Glass Manufactory, Konigsbau, Festaalbau, Ludwig's Kirche, Basilica, Maria Hilf, Royal Chapel, Ludwig Strasse, Feldernhalle, Bavaria, Walhalla, Temple of Liberation—the last two near Ratisbon—Pompaianeum and Donan, Marie Canal, besides many statues and monuments, such as the obelisk on the Carolinenplatz, cast in metal from conquered cannon. His son, Maximilian II, reigned from 1848 to 1864. His attention and efforts seem to have been principally directed to the advancement of science, though he was not behind in the beautifying and practical development of the city. To him it owes the Cornmarket, the Crystal Palace, Railway Station, Old Winter Garden, Lying-in Hospital, Physiological Institute, Maximilian Strasse, Riegerung, Bavarian National Museum, Maximilian Bridge, or rather two bridges in one over the Isar, Maximilianeum, Gasteig Park, etc.; certainly sufficient evidence that his comparatively short reign of sixteen years was not frittered away. This king must have been noble, indeed, and specially qualified for a great and good ruler; such affection and reverence cling to his memory. Only last week I read a most touching reminiscence of him recalled by his physician and spiritual father, Dr. R. von Reindl, who was one of the few present in attendance when the king was on his death-bed. At five o'clock of the day he died, in the morning, the great bell of the Frauen Kirche was rung to summon all Munich to pray for the sick monarch. Hearing it in his sick-room, he asked, "Dear Reindl, what holy day is this?" "Sire," he replied, "the Bavarian people are praying for their king." He spoke again: "Ah, am I so near my end? Well, I am ready. I have always wished the best for my people, and never intentionally injured anyone. I ask forgiveness from all." There is something sublime in such an exhibition of resignation and humility. He was not yet fifty-four years of age, and in the prime of his powers and usefulness. Among the many monuments of Munich, his, at the end of Maximilian Strasse, is the grandest and most imposing.

He stands in his coronation robes, holding the charter, on a pedestal of granite and syenite, around which are beautiful figures representing Peace, Religion, Justice and Strength. It bears the simple, perfect inscription, "Erected by his faithful people."

The present king, Ludwig II, has, it is said, carried out some of the plans of his father, and is as much given to building castles as was Charlemagne. Doubtless you are familiar with his reputation for eccentricity, as it has a world-wide publicity. So extreme has been its exhibition, it has obtained for him the title of "the mad king." It is difficult to get a fair estimate of him; but if he is mad, there is, like Hamlet's, "method in his madness." He held his own against the Kaiser in the adjustment of United Germany; would not be swallowed by the whale, though he was such a little fish. He works daily for hours on state matters, and signs no papers without his full personal examination. He is credited with being so shrewd that neither his ministers nor others can get the advantage. "No fooling him to the top o' his bent." He is kind-hearted and benevolent—gave forty thousand marks, against the Kaiser's fifteen thousand, to the recent sufferers from the inundations; and he seems to keep watch for, and is swift to reward, any special exhibition of merit in science or art. All this on the one hand; on the other there is quite as much. He lives his own life, regardless of everything but his own will and tastes. He absents himself from his capital. He lives alone, leading a singularly isolated life—he would seem to be a misanthrope. He does the most anomalous things. Here is a specimen: one of his residences (Residenz is the name of the royal palaces here), six miles from the city, is interesting for its pictures and extensive and fine grounds. He spent some weeks there last summer, and won the idolatrous worship of the villagers and country folk around, by mingling with them and treating them with the utmost kindness. One of the picture galleries is called "the Gallery of Ancestors," its walls being hung with portraits of five hundred of the Wittelsbach house. Well, he ordered a magnificent banquet laid in this gallery, calling it "the feast of the ancestors;" a plate for each and a tall wax candle for each; and he spent the night at table, the only living guest and banqueter!

It is to be hoped the long line of unsubstantial shadows of the house of Wittelsbach were able to appreciate the honor conferred on them.

In personal appearance, he has been an extraordinarily handsome man; tall, a head and shoulders above most men; symmetrical, of superb, real kingly bearing; with a finely shaped head, rich masses of brown hair, and splendid, large, dark, expressive eyes. I have seen fine portraits of him at different periods from seventeen or eighteen years of age till now. In all, he is a strikingly handsome man. He was here the first of November, after an absence of six months; remained two weeks. I saw him twice in his carriage. He is growing exceedingly stout—too much so for my taste—but still shows what he has been. What sharp-tongued Frenchman was it who said, "*un homme d'esprit meurt, mais n'engraisse pas?*" How much more applicable to looks than wit!

Oh! I must not forget to tell you that this puzzling king is a poet and a man of varied and most exquisite taste. I have the promise of seeing a little volume of his poems, a very few copies of which have found their way into the hands of the officers of his household, friends of these German friends with whom I am domiciled. They are said to be full of a melancholy sweetness and pathos. His taste is shown in the furnishing as well as in the architecture of his palaces. Everything from the draperies to the tiniest bit of bric-a-brac in every apartment, in all these palaces, he has built or is building, is from his own designs. Those who have been fortunate enough to see them rave over their rare and wonderful beauty and richness. Will you begin to think, "Isn't that all; can there be anything more?" I have not told the best! This strange, shrewd, "mad" Bavarian king has a spotless reputation. With so much that is admirable, might it not be hoped that in the course of time, the eccentricities will disappear and the "fittest survive?" The prominent feature in summing up these Bavarian kings is their unselfishness. Mere selfish gratification seems to have had no place in their lives. All their faculties, energies, time, revenues and efforts were devoted to a beneficent development and improvement of their realm. Such men should rule whether "born to the purple or not."

So endeth my letter on the kings. Sometime I may take you with me to their palaces. We can go whenever we wish; so can the humblest subject in their kingdom. I saw on last Saturday one, thin and old, and poorly clad, standing before a picture in one of the royal corridors leading from the Cologne suite to the state apartments. She seemed to be enjoying it quite as much as I was. She had her market basket on her arm and was on her way home: it was full. All she had to do was to make choice of her church, or her king's palace, or she may have gone to both; each was alike open to her. How much the graciousness of such custom is to be commended!

L. G. C.

Munich, January 2, 1883.

MUNICH.

HERE is your first letter in the new year. I have been giving you a rest. I did a little sum in arithmetic myself, and that addition of letters looked so formidable it drove me into sandwiching this interval. Has the experiment been satisfactory, do you ask? Only in proving to myself that I can be unselfish. I had a friend in Philadelphia once who had the scathingest tongue. He used to say: "All women like and seek more or less martyrdom." Maybe and maybe. I know I said to myself: "He has to answer all those. Think of such a tax! Because you are away from home and yearn so for news, you have been thoughtless. He has many correspondents; he has much to do. Think of how you may be interfering! Perhaps he sits up o' nights, or heralds the dawn to get you in. If—but never mind how. Your conscience has been stirred; you'll be good; you are penitent; you'll bring forth works meet for repentance; you'll give him a rest!"

I have been good. I've done my penance

beautifully. I know I have, for I feel like—an archangel. But—look out for the next three weeks! It will be anomalous perfection of conduct if I do not, like the most exemplary, "reformed drunkard," give this self-imposed restraint a treat a day! Best be looking around for a bookkeeper—graduate of Bryant Commercial College—to help foot up the columns then! And what a quick transit you will make into the beauties of multiplication—how the twenties will multiply! Oh! I can tell you, if you are going "to keep count" on me, I'll see to it you'll have enough to do. Now, aren't you scared? Your letter is beautiful—a prose poem! I know one when I come across it. Did you ever read "Prue and I?" One passage, that about your Spanish castle, recalls "My Chateaux." I kept that for years where I could turn to it and read it over and over again. A little less, and your letter might have slipped alongside. If you had only not been as poetical over that Thanksgiving turkey and pudding! How could you substitute them for "nectar and ambrosia?" Yes, I may submit gracefully to the "durance vile" of your Spanish castle; may lean from its windows, meeting more than half-way the smell of the poppies—to be steeped in blissful forgetfulness by it! but not shackles of adamant; not

or,
"The wind-blown breath of the tossing flower;"

or,
"the scent of the sweet tuberose,
The sweetest thing for scent that blows;"

"Nord and cassia's balmy smells."

No; not anything of all the sweetest and strangest lures and fetters you know can ever get me into your Paradise, with its Thanksgiving turkey every day. Goodness! what a material creature is your being of two hundred avoirdupois! How different your Paradise is from mine, which is

"a fairy vision
Of those gay creatures of the elements
That in the colors of the rainbow live
And play i' the plighted clouds,"

and who share the feasts of humming-birds, butterflies, and gold fishes. Ah! you have never split honeysuckle bells for those dainty drops of honey in their depths! You have never hovered over the spiced fumes of pinks! If you wish for an apotheosis, to be caught up into a more etherial sphere, get a vase of gold fishes and watch how they live on air, and learn "how much too much" the lord of creation *eats*. I have one—here in a vase set in a thicket of tropical plants—the prettiest creature! I call him my "Flash of Gold." He goes for a week at a time on just "air, thin air," filtered through the pellucid element in which he sports or that element itself. His health, activity, grace and symmetry are simply perfect. Thank you for the little gem, "Summer Love." I have done your bidding, read it and read it again. It is worth it "for passionate remembrance' sake." I made acquaintance with your friend "a many years agone" through another little poem, which is still in the portfolio I left behind. It was a *vade mecum*, and as sacred as if it had been written for only me. I miss it now occasionally and wonder how I overlooked it. I never have seen him—the author, "who builded better than he knew"—I hope he has not killed his boys with such weight of names. To bear them, they should have stuff to send them "a pitch beyond the flight" of common men. I wish you *had* gone to A—— P——'s wedding; then you could have told me all about it, and, besides, given me all the old town's gossip. When you choose, do you know, you can furnish forth "a capital dish of that cate!" And who doesn't like it? Even Carlyle gives us leave:

"Gossip springing free and cheery from the human heart is infinitely better than inane, grey haze." I am quite satisfied about "the other side of the river" since your last. Remember, it came after my letter of the 12th was gone. Mrs. M——, my cousin A——, is indeed a divine musician and one of the most brilliantly-gifted women I have ever known. I am glad you met her, and sorry you did not meet oftener. I had a letter from Miss B—— the same day I received your last, the first for a long time. Useless to enjoin me to "write often" under such circumstances. I am not like the stars that scintillate in the vast silence and darkness; I must have response. The dear woman has, however, had more sufficient cause for the prolonged interval. Such trials of sickness, nursing, and death—one of those heart-crushing experiences that every life must know at some period or other. I am so glad I had written several days before her letter came. I can say nothing because there is no escape from her present life; the claims are those of blood, and duty, and love, and "though 'the way leads over the burning marl,' her feet must tread therein." I pray, however, it may not last much longer. If she were stronger, I should feel less solicitude. Do *you* please write to her as often as you can. Your words will do her great good; they will give her momentary forgetfulness of that wearing round of duty—some refreshing "surcease of care." I wish she had been well enough to stay with me; but she was not. I was terrified at times thinking "if she should die." You know she would not have come except on my account. When she seemed breaking down, the sense of responsibility was beyond words. My disappointment in the whole plan has been one of the most bitter in my life. Had all gone as we thought it would, ours would have been as I said, "an ideal trip."

You did not say a word about Christmas. Have you erased it from your calendar? Seems to me you might have said to me at least, "A pleasant Christmas; a good New Year." Why didn't you? I had such a unique and beautiful time, I want to tell you something about it. Have I mentioned that I am in a German family? The mother, three daughters and a young son of sixteen constitute the little circle. We three are the only outsiders. My friend and myself were taken possession of to help decorate the Christmas tree that reached to the ceiling. This was Sunday after-dinner work.

We helped with a will. At five it was "a thing of beauty," of dazzling beauty, if it did owe its sheen and glitter to tinsel and icicles of glass. Then we were dismissed. At seven, we sat down to our usual supper. The frau-mutter was invisible and the doors of the saal (salon) closed and locked on the inside. We were not allowed to quit the table till 8:30 o'clock, when the locked doors were thrown wide open, the portiéres thrust aside, and we were invited to enter. We rushed! Every kind of light and color made such a blaze we could not see for a moment. Five tables of presents, mine being one, and full of such pretty things. Maybe I'll show them to you when I come home. Among them "The Niebelungenlied," in German! After admiring everything to the full, a pretty and tempting table appeared as if by magic, and we sat down to a delicious collation. We lingered over it till eleven, then we went to church to see a specially-fine and solemn service. Never did I witness anything so strange, spectral, and weird. It lasted an hour. At the conclusion, we made the circuit of the altars to see their decorations. One had the Christmas child (a beauty of a wax doll) in a cradle of roses. Men, women, and children were dropping on their knees to it. It seemed to do them a world of good. We came home to find another table awaiting us with beer and coffee in addition to the other good things. How long we sat over that I cannot say, but Christmas wishes were exchanged long before we broke up. I don't mind acknowledging it looks as if we "made a night of it." The ensuing week was too full to even touch on, so I skip to New Year's Eve, when we had another characteristic time. There was a German New Year's Eve banquet, dishes never served at any other time. One was a salad, a kind of Salmagundi compounded of every known edible and condiment—at least I can't think of anything that was left out! After several courses of such came all kinds of—oh! goodies and goodies—cakes, nuts, candies, fruits—oh! everything, and a great, magnificent punch-bowl was borne in in a kind of state procession. But didn't I hope it was eggnogg! It wasn't, though; it was a "Burgundy punch." Well, we ate, nibbled cakes, crunched candies, cracked nuts and jokes, and drank toasts standing, and clinking glasses till we rang out the Old and in the New Year. I wasn't a success in the drinking, "'pon honor," but you ought to have seen how soon I caught the trick of clinking. Our hostess taught us. You see that was poetry, rythm, the sweetest, softest music like Swiss bell ringing! The punch, I take it was an innocuous drink. Nobody's head was lost if everybody's tongue was found! These kindly German people, these pleasant, social customs, "this golden, fair enchanted life in the valley of Bohemia"—how I shall miss them when I go! Alas! I am beginning to flutter my wings. Paris or Vienna next en route to Italy. So sorry to leave, but I want to see them too. Now, if you were only in Italy, what a pair of tramps we would be!

I am waiting to hear what you think of "the counterfeit presentment." It does not show the faded roses and the false teeth (I kept my mouth shut), but the frosted locks and the crow's feet would n't be left out. Remember to send it back if it does not suit.

No. 21 or 22. Pshaw! don't let's keep count—" The fair penitent."

L. G. C.

Munich, January 15, 1883.

MUNICH.

I THINK I have written to you from this city before. Do you remember? Well, no need for alarm. I have no intention of treating you to a second dish of my raptures.

Yours of September 8th came to hand some days ago. My promptness in reply is meant to point no moral. If people prefer being laggards, I have no objection; only *I* am not of that ilk, and must be taken in kind. You know I can't tell a lie. I tried my best to fix up an innocent one—the kind that cheats oneself into thinking it not a lie at all. The ingenious sophism would not work. Yet I have done it many a time. What is the matter with me? My heart is troubled. I am afraid of myself; afraid for myself; afraid I am getting too good for this world. I hope you are not praying over me as a dear little girl I knew over her baby brother, that all the world was praising. "Why do you pray so for Arthur to be one of the good little children, Sprite?" "Oh! because all the good little

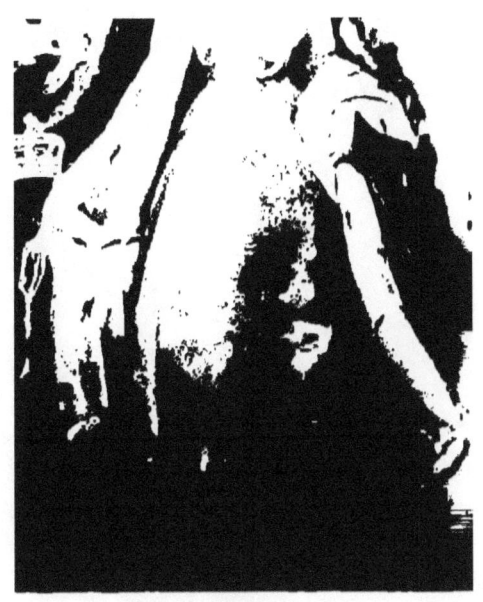

Queen Louise.

children die and go to heaven; and then he'll be *out of my way.*"

Well, I just read your letter outright. That's all there is about it.

So let all the world keep the cotton out of their ears. It has the secret; so have the cousins! I don't believe you know what a readable letter you wrote. It was n't a bit of trouble to make the meaning plain; and for the mere reading, why every syllable just came tripping from the tongue. And long before I got to the announcement, the ladies exclaimed: "Oh! we know what he is going to tell—his age." I don't see why you want to keep it such a secret, anyhow. To be sure *sixty* is n't a boy's age, but then neither is it an antediluvian's. Dear me! Only think if you had been "the prehistoric man," or even Methuselah! Then you might have well prepared to whisper it into the soundless silence. Somehow you keep all their names to yourself. It makes it very awkward for me when I need to use them. See how inconsiderate you are. Do you think that sort of treatment " good breeding!" If you do, I'll give you a new version.

I don't feel sure about your last scintillation—that is, that it was ever started across the sea. You have not mentioned it before, and you had plenty of chances. Instead of crossing ours did n't it scintillate "all of a suddint" after you heard of ours.

Be a "living monument" of moral courage that owns up—when cornered! *Be.*

I had a letter from Miss B—— last week. She is in Paris, and wished me to join her and go to Sweden and Norway. Had it been two months earlier it would have been the very thing to do; but it is now too late for the midnight sun. When I go I want to see that too. Do you know she is a writer spoken of as the delightful authoress of "A Trip to Scandinavia," "The Midnight Sun," and "Travels through Russia and the Orient"? I don't believe you dreamed what she was when you saw her. You would have been less *presumptuous!* You have done it. Tremble and quake as you recall your audacity. What is left for you to do next time? I have had a letter from the other Miss B——too, recently. Do you write often to her? It is worth any one's while to wring her letters from her. Such weather as she wrote of! It made one think of the "Garden of Eden."

As for coming home, I don't see my way to that yet; perhaps in the Spring. I do not bind myself to go or to stay; only I wish to go to Spain, Greece and the Orient first. Once back, then I doubt if I shall ever come again. Chimney corner days are at hand. We are meantime enjoying the world about us. This city is brimful of interest, you know.

Yesterday was a grand gala day. I must have written to you of the October Fest, a mixed exposition of the peasants and common classes, agricultural, cattle, horse-racing, games, and side-shows. It is held in some meadows at the foot of the great statue; lasts about two weeks. Open on Sunday, and the second Sunday is the one set apart for the attendance of the court. The late king, poor, mad, gifted, handsome Louis, omitted this. He kept up no customs that exacted his appearance in public. The regent announced his intention to resume. This meant a full attendance of all the royal family in all their gorgeousness. It attracted an immense crowd reckoned at 70,000. We were of it. The day was perfect, crystal clear, and just cool, just warm enough. All sorts of costumes, equipages, and human beings, the last a well-dressed, well-behaved, most amiable mass.

The regent came in an open carriage with six horses and jockeys in brilliant trappings, preceded and followed by a fine body-guard. His three sons and two nephews came in open carriages likewise, but with only four horses. Some ducal kinsmen in two-horse carriages; ambassadors and government officers in all their state. It was a most brilliant spectacle. I wish I had time to tell you all about it.

We had a day last week at the Augsburg six months' Exposition just closing. The show was, of course, a "Centennial" on a small scale; the old city was ravishingly quaint, medieval and interesting.

But a four o'clock tea at the apartments of an officer in the army, who has married a young German friend of mine, was beyond words. "The linen closet!" If you had seen it, you would have bewailed your bachelor fate. The "tea" was a drink fit for the gods, with a *soupçon* of —— *rum* in it.

L. G. C.

Munich, October 4, 1886.

The Historic Windmill.

PARIS.

WELL, here I am at last in Paradise! I was a long time on the way, but I would not have back one moment. To paraphrase dear, simple-hearted, child-like Hans Christian Anderson, "My journey has been a lovely dream, happy, and full of incident."

I left Munich two weeks ago alone, for a twenty-four hours' railway trip, in a mixture of foreign countries and a medley of foreign languages that would have swallowed me up in inextricable confusion, but for the wise precautions I had taken to fend it off. I made requisitions in every direction and on every available person on almost as extensive a scale as the Kaiser might if he were going in for a big war; the American consul and all my other acquaintances—their name was not "legion"—all being called upon. I had a royal escort to the station— three ladies and Mr. S—— placed me in the care of the "guard" (conductor), who spoke French and German. His fluency in both I'll own was a trifle aggravating. My friends had put me in my "carriage" (sleeper), which was elegant and commodious, such as only princes and princesses and the like are in the habit of using. I had it all to myself. How I wish that Tower of Babel incident had happened on some other planet. Then they all smothered me with kisses, and the dear, young fräuleins with tears. The warning shriek sent them tumbling over each other to get off the train. Handkerchiefs were waved from the platform, and oh! in a flash I was out in the universe of moonlight and solitude, cut off from all I know. But, having obeyed the instructions of my special advisers, the American consul and others, not to have a courier, I felt no anxiety. Said the A. C., "Tip the guard." Ditto, said Mr. S——, "Tip the guard," and "Tip the guard," chimed in No. 3. And on my order to that effect, said Mr. S——, young America, Harvard graduate! "I've made it bully with the guard." So that guard didn't mean to bear the weight on his conscience without rendering a fair equivalent of service. In he came popping every few minutes to say something in that dreadfully fluent German. If he thought I was not understanding fast enough, resorting to French (and this is a most mortifying admission); when both seemed failing, he tripped into the most ludicrously despairing pantomime! At bedtime he put a crimson shade over my lamp and bade me "good-night" with that exquisite French politeness that has not its match in the world, charging me to call him if I needed anything. But—the chilly little bed he had made for me—Ugh! It made me shiver just to look at it. Think of it, linen sheets and one spread after my German nest of down—a bed of it under and another over me.

Fortunately, I think the earth never saw a lovelier night, a full moon and that clear, keen air that tells "Jack Frost" is busy; and the pretty country slipping past so fast in the dazzling white light. I sat up, of course. Towards morning it grew "cold, very cold." It was ruthless in me, but I stripped that bed of its one cover to wrap up in. When we ran into Strassburg at five and got out for breakfast, I just roasted myself by the great, generous fire. My waiter spoke English. I crossed his hand with that douceur, "a silver shilling," in England, mark, in Germany. Believe me, the sweetest sounds ever syllabled by human tongue are those of one's own vernacular. On the frontier, we changed from German to French cars, from the luxurious warmth of the former to the comfortless cold of the latter; the one heated by invisible registers, the other by a tube of hot water laid on the floor—merely a poor foot-warmer. I was never more tired of a journey, all because of the cold; therefore never so glad to see the end.

When I jumped out of the carriage at the Gare de L'Est, you need not be told how glad I was to find a relative awaiting me. He took me to the Grand Hotel, the largest and most fashionable in Paris, and after I was rested, out on the balcony attached to show me the Rue des Capucins by gas-light, lamp-light, moon-light, and star-light. I was overwhelmed with the sight, speechless at such a brilliant spectacle—millions, it seemed, of lights in every possible arrangement. This winter has been so rainy, I am glad I came no sooner. I shall be away by the middle of the month to Italy, and return again to Paris later.

The view from my private balcony (at a pension kept by a French lady, to which I have changed from the hotel) is charming, and the Arc de Triomphe de l'Etoile is not a stone's throw distant. I also see the great palace of Mrs. Mackey from my balcony; it is nearer than the Arc. It has a little square all to itself. She is now at Nice, and it is closed. I heard that Mr. Mackey is worth two hundred millions! Grace Greenwood is in Paris. Her daughter is pronounced by everyone to be "exquisitely beautiful."

I have seen the Hotel des Invalides, Champs de Mars, Trocadero, Passy, the loveliest suburb of homes; the Bois de Boulogne, that you know by heart, but oh! what an enchantment to know by sight; the Champs Elysées; the Place de la Concorde; the garden of the Luxembourg; the Palace de l'Étoile with the grand Arc de Triomphe, the largest, they say, in the world; the Madeleine; Chapelle Expiatoire; and the afternoon at the Gobelins, looking at those wonders of wool, silk, gold and silver, wrought in such patience "by the most practiced eye" by men's fingers never allowed to demean themselves by other work of whatever kind; and the Champs Elysees on Sunday afternoon! This last is the great moving human spectacle. I have seen nothing like it but Hyde Park on that gala-day of "The meet of the four-in-hands." Such countless lines of carriages in the street! Looking ahead I could not see how we were ever going to get through the approaching host, apparently as compact and impregnable as one's idea of the advancing columns of an army. I tell you it filled me with awe. In the street I could not detect space enough for even one more carriage. One must see to comprehend how grand and imposing such a vast concourse of seething humanity is.

The weather is like our last of April. The grass is thick and green, and from three to five inches high. The flower-beds in the squares are full of flowers. As one walks or drives, whiffs of sweet violets are constantly blown to you. At least one great flower-shop greets the delighted eye every half-square. The sunshine is a dazzle most of the time. I must stop, but will write more at an early date.

L. G. C.

Paris, February 4, 1883.

PARIS.

OH, DEAR! I don't know where to begin. It seems an age since I wrote; "in point of fact" it has been only—oh! I shan't go into calculations and dates. Figures are such unmanageable little demons I cut them long ago. There is no such thing as getting round them. They are so fair and square and exact and relentless, I throw up my hands and give up without struggle when it comes to a contest with them. Let me see; I must make a beginning somewhere. Where did I leave off, I wonder? Does it matter? How can it, seeing I am not "a newspaper correspondent," or writing for fame or "filthy lucre," or for anything in the "wide, wide world" that can be attributed to a higher impulse than natural depravity? For between ourselves, to be really honest, I do believe I am writing simply and solely to—nag you! Why? Oh, just because "a woman's reason." It is not only argument, but it overcomes all logic, which, from your superior sphere of immensity, being a bachelor, you have not found out. Just look out when you get your supplemental hemisphere, and think of these words! They are a lot of nonsense to you now; they will be the quintessence of wisdom to you then. But I am not going to let you any further into the secrets of that blissful "two in one existence." Go and find out for yourself, "old boy." In Paradise! Write a poem on those words; they seem meant for me. Well, I have been in this, "the Paradise of all good Americans," for two weeks plus. Somehow I think I can find a better one for my soul, but it is a tiptop place for one still in the body.

I came from Paris *all alone* one lovely moonlight night and sunshiny day. The trip had a smack of royalty in it. I chartered a wagon lit (a "sleeping-car," as *we* say), and bribed the garde (conductor), and otherwise bestowed myself "as only princes and princesses do in this country," said the pleasant German people with whom I had been domiciled so long. "Oh!" said I, "*I* am a princess; we are all princesses in America, *or can be*"—the last little clause *sotto voce*. My "wagon" was all crimson, velvet and mahogany, and looked so glowy when my cavalier shrouded the lamp, a generous one in size and esthetic in its finish of antique bronze, in a crimson shade, I thought it was heated to midsummer warmth; but did n't I find out to the contrary before morning! And the thin, chilly little French couch after my German nest of down—will I ever forget it? Every time I glanced at it, it just resolved the whole me— body, mind and spirit—into one big shiver. Thanks to the glorious full moon, that could not put out Orion though, there was ample entertainment outside, so I sat up all night. It did not seem long till that freezing period just before dawn set in; then all my wraps, and the little bed's *one cover* added to them, could n't make me warm.

You can guess I was glad when we ran into Strassburg at five, and I was conducted to a great, bright, comforting fire and a delicious hot breakfast. My special waiter talked English, too, and I did n't give him a rest for the hour we tarried there. My blessed native tongue! Take my word for it, till you prove for yourself, the sweetest sounds human ear can catch are those of one's own vernacular. The German cars were heated by invisible registers and were the perfection of comfort, but at Avricourt, the frontier, we changed into French, and their heating apparatus was a flat zinc tube laid on the floor, "a mere foot warmer." "I kept chilling," as they say in ague countries, all the rest of the day, notwithstanding an Italian gentleman who spoke four languages, English being one, and two French gentlemen who spoke French only, devoted themselves to securing my comfort. The delicacy of the adjustment of their attentions I shall never forget—to the extreme of courtesy, but never verging on obtrusiveness. Well, the long, wearing day came to an end, and Paris and my uncle met me. But—this is why I told you all the above—such a dreadful cold as the trip and change from German comfort to French chilliness and cheerlessness gave me! I have been fighting it ever since. It is accompanied with an excess of deafness. And now you can account for all my viciousness.

I have had "a pretty good time" though, notwithstanding. Have been to a beautiful dinner party, where I met eighteen very agreeable Americans and two or three French people. Have made other pleasant acquaintances, and "got in" a reasonable amount of "sight-seeing." The weather till yesterday and to-day has been all sunshine and April-like in temperature. The grass is from three to four inches high, thick and green in the squares, gardens and Bois de Boulogne, and the flower-beds are full of flowers. I have bundled up equal to an Esquimau and had several "outings," leaving my cold to its own devices. And I have—*"honor bright"*—fallen in love. Perfectly ridiculous and absurd in one of my age! but I could not keep it. He is *so* handsome, so elegant, so genial, so witty, so entertaining—so everything! I wasn't thinking of such a catastrophe, and I did not know what was the matter till the mischief was done. Don't pity my infatuation. I glory in it. He is "worth millions," and 81+. You ought to see us enjoy each other. I'll tell you more about him some time.

Paris does not overwhelm me as London did, because, I suppose, I did not see it *first;* nor does it charm me as Munich did, perhaps because I have so much Dutch blood in my veins against not one drop of French. The parts I have seen do not give it a distinctive character; it is rather cosmopolitan, like our great cities, than foreign. I had a lovely half-day—nothing seems to be done here till after the 12 o'clock breakfast—at Napoleon's monument, the grandest I have seen; the Hotel des Invalides, with its church and armory and picturesquely dilapidated ruins of human beings; the Trocadero; Passy, a charming suburb of homes; and so through a part of the Bois de Boulogne and the Champs Elysees home. Another, I spent at the manufactory of the *Gobelins,* those tapestries as immortal as the frescoes of Angelo and Raphael. Some of them are worked from express designs by the latter. Think of six square inches a day being a full-grown man's daily task! Such a respectable-looking body of men as they are, too! They are raised for that special work, and their hands are not permitted to degrade themselves by contact with any other. Yet another at a Pompeian palace—meant to be an exact reproduction of the villas of that buried city. It is a gem of unique and exquisite beauty, and I broke one of the commandments; for I could not help coveting my neighbor's possessions. It is full of Story's (*our* Story) statuary.

One statue, Saul, is in tinted marble, a grand, majestic old man, and certainly in some respects a triumph of the chisel's art, but I am not quite sure I indorse the tinting. No satisfaction can be complete. There was a number of imposing female statues; their names are at the base in *Greek characters,* which I know. What I did not know, nor any of the party, was the English of those names! I ground my teeth and "vowed a vow"—when I die and am resurrected, I mean to be mistress of every language under the sun *or* abolish all but one. There shall never be another Tower of Babel experiment on the same planet with myself— never! One of the paintings on the wall of the picture gallery was a haunting one—a turbulent ocean, a cloudy sky; not high in the heavens a thinner mass of cloud through which the moon shone with sufficent strength to cast a wake of spectral light athwart those heaving surges. "Solitude" was the name. I could not keep my eyes from it. I have seen just such a night, and felt in all its force the dreary, weird solitude of it. Do I make you see it? Shut your eyes and try. I go from here to Italy in a few days.

L. G. C.

Paris, February 8, 1883.

PARIS.

HERE again, after six months' absence—six months only! How to believe that! Why, I seem to have lived cycles and cycles; seem to be not one, just one small, insignificant I, but dozens and dozens of myself. Yes, even sometimes have an enormous delusion that the little nobody who went away suffered a not-sea, but an no, not-earth—What then? Ah! I have it: tourist change into something strange, grand, glorious (it must out), goddess-like! Was ever presumption so immense and so absurd? Well, *I* am not responsible for it, but the *experiences*. Could any mortal go through such and escape the same scath?

September 2d. If good intentions were the same sort of masters that czars, emperors, the great mogul, the sublime porte, *et id omne genus* are, or have been—what a lot of things come under that last pathetic head—this letter would have been finished and on the way to you. But there is such a throng of hindering duties got themselves mixed up in my affairs, I really don't know what moment I may be ruthlessly torn from the performance of what I wish to do to that I wish —still more to do! Such is woman's—

September 3d. Just there I was torn off again after I don't know how many feminine raps at my door and feminine heads bobbing in, and, worst of all, each of them supplied with that rabidest of all tongues, a feminine one! (Let alone a woman for a just estimate of her own sex!) Don't that last dozen lines show "confusion worse confounded" from some cause? You have no leave to indulge in mental comment, such as, "Perhaps, my lady, that unspiritual circumstance was in your own state of mind, without any outside pressure to develop it." And so don't you dare. Truth is, I was in the superlative degree of calmness, collectedness, clearness, comprehensiveness, like clouds that have gathered their quota of electricity, the inevitable "next thing" being "the most brilliant display of fireworks of the season." Any letter heretofore would have been a battery of "spent balls," an eruption of mere dead cinders. There! that's what you would have gotten, what you have missed, because of those hindering goddesses. "The more's the pity."

I glance up at that last broken sentence,

"Such is woman's —." What was to follow, I am as much at a loss to recall as a panic-stage, I mean—struck, debutante of the boards. Oh! for "a prompter." Can't you come to the rescue? I will "most graciously permit." And do you know, even now when I have double-locked (both doors and *ears*) myself in for this blessed privilege of communion with a "choice fellow-being," these pages are bound to be tossed off with the lightning-like rapidity of a printing-press of the latest patent, not only with all modern improvements, but those of the future too! For somebody is coming directly to *dejeuner* with me, another specimen of feminine attributes, that of being equal to inviting herself, being not the least. She will claim me for the rest of the day. And that's the way it will be.

You will see,
And alas! and alas! for this letter to thee,
If it be not writ a la electricity,
Or by some still more potent diablerie!

There's a flash of inspiration for you, which reminds me I had a feminine compliment yesterday among those other feminine impositions. If it had been of masculine origin, how different would have been the animus of the

The Old Lion, Lucerne.

"return-thanks." She said, it must be true if one woman could bestow such words on another, so you need n't try to put a pin in my balloon. "Mrs. Collins is always *inspired.*" I had just "made a remark" as innocent as "a natural" (Scotch for idiot) of any intention to soar above "the dead level." Think of my sudden inflation. In all your kite-flying days, you never gave one such "a bully send-off." You may be sure I did not allow myself to "flop down" by opening my mouth except for "rations" the rest of the day. But was I ever "in the whole course of my long life" whirled about in such an eddy of nonsense? I can't account for it, unless on the principle of counter-irritation, because writing to you who are so lavish of "good, sound sense." Bite and wait for your own turn. I am applying soothing lotions already in anticipation of the crunching your reply will give me. How I'll wish I had not *then.* Well, now I may as well have out "my dance on a fiddle-string."

I left off at Lucerne. I wish I could remember what I told you of that lovely week there. I shan't venture on more than a word for fear of repeating myself. But I want you to know, if I did not tell you, what a hold that "lion" has taken. You know about it;

that it is carved in a grotto out of the natural sandstone in the face of the grand cliff, the crest of which is fringed with overhanging trees. It is reclining, dying, transfixed by a broken lance, and protecting with its poor, helpless paw the shield of France with its Bourbon Lily. Anything more noble and pathetic I cannot conceive. It made my heart ache as the Dying Gladiator did. I wanted to get near enough to take its head in my lap and stroke it, and chafe its paw with my hands, and somehow make it feel my human sympathy. Indeed, it is a miracle "in kind," that dead stone can be wrought into forms that so move one. The wonder of this is that it is a *lion*—the lord of the brute creation, it is true—but not a human being in a lion's form. The qualities expressed are those tested in our intercourse with that "lower order of creation," affection, sense of trust, faithfulness unto death. You don't know how often I think of him, and yearn to him as to a living suffering creature, that majestic creation of one of my fellow beings. Oh! sometimes I take a most reverential pride in my race. Who was it—Dr. Holland—who said, "It is a great thing to be a man?" One must agree now and again. I shan't linger on Lucerne now. Hereafter, may be. From there

here will have to be a skeletonized sketch. You can't divine the difficulty of leaving out how trying such shadowy limning is to such an effusive creature as I, who have always had the dubious distinction of making not something, but *so much out of nothing, of seeing more than is ever shown.* Alas! poor me.

From Lucerne by the Schöellenen Defile and Furka Pass to the Rhone Glacier, a diligence trip from Andermat, giving many privileges in the way of fine views and other things, such as "getting up very high in the world." At last nothing but barren rocks, snow and the plucky little wild flowers, that wouldn't be beaten out of beautifying waste places as long as a cleft or cranny was found to give them a foothold. At the very highest, 7,992 feet, I could have made snow-balls with one hand and posies with the other without moving. I saw the great glacier from almost every point, and in such a glow of sunshine as can only be transcended in some other world. From it to Visp. Here I had my first "mule ride," *on horseback, with a guide to lead it.* This for four hours; then a blessed exchange to an open carriage, which in as many more hours brought us to Zermatt, at the foot of the Matterhorn.

Here the windows of my room just framed that curious freak of rock and snow, and I saw its transfiguration at dawn without moving my head from my pillow. Give me due credit though for the early wakefulness that won me that spectacle. First, in the wink of an eye, one glowing, burning golden ruby spot—the tip of the horn struck by the first gleam in the crystal of dawn; then it spread downward like the suffusion of a blush to where its base seemed resting on a dark pine-covered mountain; and behold! the whole gigantic horn a dazzling mass of that fervid glow. You can guess Beauty in the fairy story did not lie stiller or more breathless under her spell of enchantment.

Then I had my second mule-ride, this time a sure-enough mule, to make the ascent of the Gorner Grat. I don't know what you know about it, but I am bound to tell you something at least of what I know. Just here I think I'll confess to a singular hallucination; *it seems to me that nothing I have been seeing was ever seen before.* My analysis of this has only gone far enough to convince me there is no egotism, self-conceit or anything "on a lower range of feeling" in this, only that innocent, unsophisticated child-feeling over an experience out of its common way. This is a ridge of rock rising in the center of a vast hollow surrounded by a vaster amphitheater of snow-peaks and glaciers, the former including the Matterhorn, Monte Rosa, etc., the latter numbering eleven. It is the sublimest spectacle my eyes have rested on. Retracing to Visp, then by rail along the Rhone to Leuk, whence by open carriage again to Leukesbad to make the passage of the Gemmi.

Leukesbad is the place where they do the spectacular bathing, remaining in the baths for hours at a time, and to beguile the tediousness thereof having floating tables on which are placed books, papers, games or refreshments—the public admitted to see what good times can be got in that way. Also there is a great curiosity in the neighborhood; a little village of a most aspiring turn of mind has built itself like an eagle's eyrie on the most inaccessible perch it could find, 8,895 feet high. The way to it is by a pathway or stairway of ladders fastened into the precipitous face of the mountains. The guide-book does not recommend a trial of it to persons liable to dizziness, and says the descent is more difficult than the ascent. It says also, however, that the view from the grotto at the end of the second ladder will repay the climber. You can guess into what climber's head that "put notions." Yes, she stole off there Sunday morning, "all alone by herself," took the measure of the feat and feet, laid aside ulster, umbrella and guide-book, and went up like a beast on all fours, and down like a crawfish. Alas! that you can never know the comfort and elation of having done it.

The passage of the Gemmi was another bona fide mule ride. I had heard so much about the precipitousness and the danger of the climb, my heart had been in my mouth whenever I thought of it for days before. Nothing but moral cowardice prevented the physical cowardice of — backing out. Were you to taunt me with "You couldn't do it again," a la Tom Sawyer, to the comrade who had just licked him (by the skin of his teeth), I'd follow his example and *not try*. Imagine, as far as in you lies, a mule-ride up a tree or a steep spiral staircase; above, sheer precipices; below, to such frightful depths, the same—two and one-half hours of that. Do you wonder I went "into retreat" at the top, if not to give thanks, surely for the precious privilege of once more drawing some long breaths? It was a five and one-half hours' mule-ride to Kandersteg at the foot on the other side. We got to our hotel at 9 p. m., and slept the sleep of the elect. Open carriage next morning to Thun; the sunshine so glorious I didn't believe *it* could ever "do it again," and every roll of the wheels bearing onward to fresh charms of earth, air and sky. From Thun to Interlaken for a week; Staubbach, drives and walks in honor of the Jungfrau, Mönch and Eiger. You know that part of the story well. All the world does it. But to no one did it ever happen what unto me there befell one wonder afternoon. At the Belvedere, atop of a pretty height which commands the best view of that trio of snow-covered beauties, a party of English ladies came in. I caught the eye of one lovely-faced, silver-haired, soft-voiced, sweet-mannered old lady; an instant exchange of bow and smile, and then much pleasant talk. At parting, she fixed her eyes on me with such a blessing-beaming look in them, and said with the clearest distinctness of those low, silver tones, "May all your walks be pleasant." I shall carry that benediction with me in every walk my feet shall tread in the future. From Interlaken to Berne, striking a *fest,* a peasant's wrestling match, set for Sunday! Fine opportunity for seeing men, women and peasants' costumes. Heard its great organ; saw the bear-clock; paid my visit of courtesy to the bears; had all its exquisite views; went to its really fine museum to see those marvelous specimens of white and black quartz-crystals, one weighing over 290 pounds and several over 200; and also "Barry," the noble St. Bernard that saved fifteen lives; and ever so much else. Then Fribourg and its lime-tree dating from 1476, its organ, and a walk that might belong to a tale of necromancy.

On to Lucerne and *the* "Lake Leman," where I went and sat in the garden in which Gibbon "wrote the conclusion of his great work." And next, Chillon! I loitered away hours there. It is the loveliest, most romantic, picturesque spot. I wish I owned it! I stayed till the sun set fire to it, the lake and the snow peaks in the background, and then saw the full moon swing into space right over it; then a long, long sigh, and the train through several stages to Vernayaz, to make another "passage" to Chamouny. Another gorge, the Gorge de Trient at V. equals that at Pfäffers. A funny little two-wheeled vehicle and a guide, and we attacked the ascent. It was n't so perilous as that of the Gemmi, but it was n't easy. We crossed a waterfall tearing down the mountain side forty-nine times over as many bridges. It was beautiful beyond the reach of words. As to giving even an idea of the innumerable beauties of that route, it would take a long summer's day to do it. There was another gorge, different, but as interesting: lovely vales, glaciers, torrents, mountains, snow peaks, cascades, almost as numerous as the hairs on your head, especially if you are inclining to baldness, and so on. At Chamouni the monarch "crowned long ago." I was a most willing worshiper at his feet. Like Mark Twain, the only ascent of him I cared to make was by telescope. But I made that of the Brerent, the next best thing. The mule ride again, with a guide at the bit; but even that did n't seem so good part of the time as my own feet, and the last half hour *had* to be done that way. It was all "of a piece" climbing up rocks and plunging over stretches of snow, while my "little hand lay lightly"—not a bit of it—with the tightest kind of a grip, as well as "confidingly," in that of my guide. He was as tender of me as a lover—more so—as for the time being we were bound to each other "for better and for worse." The Mer-de-glace came in too; not the conventional walk across; for one who had walked across the Ohio, what was that, pray? Bah! From Chamouni by diligence, in an ecstasy all the way to Geneva. There for some days, with excursions on the lake into its realms of inexplicable blue, where everything was so unreal and ethereal. I felt as if I too were a phantom, a dream, a spirit, just as little of a reality as all I was surrounded by. From Geneva here.

About that book, and your need of the aid of "good taste, judgment and scholarship," it strikes me any one who had to help that much would feel, like you, "certainly very glad when the creature was fledged." Thankee, sir; I never can bear to know what I am to have for dinner, or any other meal. That for sauce. This for earnest. Call on Miss B——. I don't know the woman who is so equal to such demand. She knows everything and has it at command. She is a long distance beyond me in such matters. This is no affectation; I mean it.

Many thanks for your charges in behalf of proper caretaking. I don't mean to break down if I can help it. Am now taking a good rest. This pension is a kind of a home—*Paris* home. I could tell some things of its kindness—yes, even petting—would show how much I have to be thankful for. The dear, good madame takes me in her arms, kisses me "from ear to ear," and, what is better, smuggles "goodies" in to me unbeknown to the others! It is too funny to see her coming with one hand covered with a napkin and the forefinger of the other on her lips! My room adjoins the salon. I take the hint. Wouldn't you? Answer.

L. G. C.

Paris, September 1, 1883.

PARIS.

YOU wrote the last day of the year and did not give me a wish for the New! Did you forget? Or do you think the custom puerile? I think I like it most heartily, even with its limitations, as are set forth in some simple lines I came across, and which you must read to make your conscience tender:

>"Tender and true, friend,
>   Yet all unavailing
>To guard or to give you
>   One gift that can bless.
>Should sorrow o'ertake
>   Or pain be assailing,
>I could not assure you
>   One trial the less.
>
>"Tender and true friend
>   As One—the all-loving,
>Whose arm will encompass
>   Should evil be near.
>Cling closely to Him—in firm
>   Faith in His proving
>Tender and true, friend,
>   Through all the New Year."

I hardly think you deserve to know what kind of time I had. You should not, only I want to tell so much I can't keep from it! I was invited to a friend's Christmas Eve tree party. She has a lovely, cozy little *apartment.* The tree was "a thing of beauty," and we guests made a jam that occupied every available square inch of standing room. The elders proved to be more childish than the children themselves, clutching their presents as generous "Old Chris." called their names, and screaming and laughing with glee at and with each other. Not the tree, nor the presents, nor the toilets, nor "the goodies" overcame me; but one superb, inexpressible specimen of the genus *homo*—an Apollo in silver locks, the frosty though kindly glow of at least seventy years. One sweeping glance sufficed for all the rest of that hilarious throng. Then I settled myself in the roomiest, deepest, sinkiest of spring-cushioned "arm-chairs," and fastened my gaze on him, to wander no more while he stayed. His wife did not come. How I did wish she had, so I could see what manner of woman had dared to mate with that grand creature.

We, my hostess and myself, had a New Year's Eve gathering. Nothing so commonplace as a tree, though. We put our heads together to devise something unique, and with that complacency characteristic of the "salt of the earth," we feel assured we were a success. Here's the program. See if you like it.

Salutatory, an *impromptu* poem, most carefully *written out beforehand* and *read* by *me*. This elicited great applause. Some amusing little characterizations by other ladies of our household. A metrical version of one of the many legends of that half-saint, half-angel of a woman—no, I don't know where the woman came in—Elizabeth of Hungary, by my hostess, who is a woman of much culture and many gifts. This was received, as it should have been, with the hush and silence of deep feeling. Music and games. Then a fishing frolic; a big pond in which every guest was invited to fish, as he or she had a *bite*, which meant a present. You can believe the fun waxed "uproarious." I was in the pond to do the biting and put the fishes on the hook; but didn't I make them tug! Some of them got so many bites they sang out, "Fishes, you needn't bite any more if you don't want to." Just on the stroke of midnight, madame recited a moan of farewell to the passing year, and in the next breath hallelujahed into the New. We all joined in at the top of our lungs, and immediately turned to each other with hearty hand-shakings, warm wishes and some kisses. Enjoying thus with much merry and kindly talk that held us together till 2 a. m. Then I spoke the lines I have copied for you and we broke up. We had our *salon* ornamented with American and French flags and evergreens from Fountainbleau.

They have a custom here of keeping "Twelfth Night." I never heard of it elsewhere. The shops are full of cakes baked expressly, each one containing "a charm," as tiny as possible. A nice china pig, or "baby" most frequently; at least I saw nothing else. If a gentleman gets the charm, he names some lady for his "queen" throughout the year; if a lady, she names her "king." I got the "baby," the weest of manikins in china. For the rest, the days come and go as swiftly as so many rays of light, scarcely here till they are gone. I have grown to begrudge the hours I have to give to sleep. I never go to bed till midnight, oftenest later, recklessly sacrificing my "beauty sleep!"—and then with the utmost reluctance, and in the main feeling as if just risen from refreshing slumber. It takes, I can tell you, all my awe of the laws of physiology to force me to that.

"Heaven of the weary head,
Bed, bed, delicious bed!"

I am not writing a book, painting a picture, composing an opera, inventing a new fangled bit of machinery, or even devising a new fashion in woman's gear! No, nor am I planning any extra wickedness; have not committed such sins as banish sleep, and yet I shun sleep. What's the trouble then? Of the most serious kind, because beyond remedy. Not all the narcotics known to science can lull me to that acceptance of "tired nature's sweet restorer" that should come as naturally as breathing and loving; it is this, it is this:

> "The years they are going,
> And ah! I am growing
> Quite old, yes, quite old, Gaffer Gray."

To think of sparing five or six hours out of twenty-four for oblivion! Would it could be otherwise. For you see "of the making of books there is no end," and readers must be found for them. None more eager or indefatigable than I. If only the days had more hours, the years more months, and sleep did not claim!

I have "Characteristics." I am your debtor for all the years to come for having written such a book. "'T would be but little could I say how much." I thank you for your publisher's promptness in sending me the book itself. It is one to have and to hold as a possession forever; to pick up and pore over, lay down and meditate on, and it has this quality of every genuine work: you cannot take much at a time; it forces you to pause and ponder, and once begun you cannot put it away for long; it claims you like a cluster of luscious grapes, one at a time, and, indeed, with pauses between, but no cessation till the bunch is finished. I shall not tell you yet which I like best, but I will tell you which I had already read and read first *before* your letter came, with its suggestion of what I would most probably prefer, and which you evidently prefer yourself—the last two! I am lending the book around. "The old beauty" has it now, and she quotes from it and uses its anecdotes, by way of illustration, always with due acknowledgment of their source. "That book I am reading of Mrs. Collins' friend." I think I never showed such unselfishness. My reward is great, though; she is charmed, and intends to get both it and "Library Notes" as soon as she goes home. I had a letter from Miss B—— since she received her copy, and she is so enthusiastic: "It is a capital book. The article on Burns I like best so far. I can't tell what rereading may do for the others. I like the drift of his mind exceedingly, and his Essays—themes, whatever they are—are unique, and the flavor is sharp and wholesome. There is nothing better I have read—that is *modern*—that reads in his direction." There! Are those not good words, indeed? May it have half the success it so richly merits!

Well, I must hurry to the finis. But first, such is the vanity of a wise woman, I am going to give you an excerpt from a love-letter that came in the same budget with yours: "I must write to you to-night, because I have been thinking and thinking of you, and wishing with all my heart I was with you, if only for these holidays; for I am sure you are like myself, and feel loneliest at this time, when all are rejoicing; but if we were together, there would be such a glow of affection that the proverbial yule log would fade by comparison, and it would take several families to supply an amount of devotion equal to ours. But let us hope we shall spend many Christmases together. I must and will have you, for I don't believe there is any one cares half so much for me, and I am sure your place in my affection is simply unapproachable to the rest of woman or mankind either."

Isn't she a darling of darlings who wrote that? And it was not Miss B——.

L. G. C.

Paris, January 1, 1884.

PARIS.

HAVE been enjoying Paris to the last degree. Weather as near perfection as this sublunary sphere allows. "The season" in full blast. Opera, theater and concerts for ourselves, these and all kinds of social entertainments, balls, parties, dinners, etc., for those who belong here and are "to the manner born."

President Grevy gives jams and crushes; the remains of the aristocracy seem most given to *the races,* which occur almost daily somewhere in and around Paris; the ambassadors give their dinners and receptions; the artists, the literateurs, the everybody, are giving their particular kind of entertainment. Arsene Houssaye gave one the other day—his "Assembly," it is called. It is peculiar, called "The Chase of the Dominos." Everybody has to wear a domino. To insure an invitation, wit, vivacity and gayety are indispensable, while, in addition, behind the masks of the women *must be beauty.* Eulogy exhausts itself on the brilliancy of the success of this host. A dreamland palace, the earth despoiled of its treasures to adorn it, an exquisite cuisine, and the incomparable host. There is no hostess. One's private character has nothing to do with it; only genius, it would seem. Such a curious medley of guests as were mentioned, Sarah Bernhardt heading the list of the feminine! I— I— wouldn't have minded being there, not "incog," but invisible! Just to have heard and seen that constellation of blazing stars. Every name was one known to fame.

I am having my chance at the musical side of Paris.

A pleasant American family, father, mother and two young lady daughters, give me the opportunity; always ready to go and eager to have me along. I am more than gratified. Will you be shocked if I admit to a Sunday afternoon concert? You know Sunday has none of our sacredness to Parisians; it is only a better, freer sort of fete day for those who have time to spare. Not all have. On my way to the concert, a week ago Sunday, I saw the house-painters busy; great wagons full of house-plunder—families changing their abodes, etc. Once in the concert-hall, "The Conservatoire," the music made everything divine, I am sure.

I do not coax impressions; so I think I may tell you, as proof of the character of the music, that at one part I seemed suddenly to have escaped from earth to that sphere we think of as Heaven. Hosts and hosts of orchestras were playing in perfect harmony with choruses joining in of countless myriads of voices, and through it all I was catching the music of the spheres. To give the least idea of how I felt, is beyond me. I was more than lifted up into "the seventh heaven." The entire audience seemed equally under the unutterable influence. It is considered the finest audience in every respect that Paris has.

Am to spend to-morrow at the Luxembourg with one of the charming, young American girls. Don't you wish you could be along? She is bright, well informed, amiable—a girl worth knowing and not too young—say about twenty-six or twenty-seven. She talks well, has an active mind, is ambitious for knowledge, and I like her. Besides, she cossets me if I feel under the weather. I think I like that best of all! Would not you? I can answer for you—yes. I am too tired for another sheet. Are you not glad?

L. G. C.

Paris, April 1, 1884.

PARIS.

WAS very glad to get your letter. It came several days ago, and I have been watching for that opportunity that never comes to those who have nothing to do to answer it. You know my trick of promptness. I never feel quite comfortable with the consciousness of a duty awaiting its performance. Consciousness or force of habit—which? *N'importe;* the result is the same. And any way, are they not interchangeable?

Yes, I am again a wandering star; or, if you will not let me go up into the empyrean, a genuine nomad. How some old Bedouin would delight in my companionship, if he could not make a big ransom off of me! But the delights of such a life are not without qualification. The passage in the Etruria was diabolical. Such pitching and tossing—why, long before it was over, I felt more like a jelly-fish than a mermaid! I was not sea-sick, but just so tired out with trying to keep my feet and my—rations—existence became loathsome. Ever so many distinguished fellow-voyagers, but I did not care even to look at them.

But—I had a beautiful week in London (not in point of weather!), seeing sights and people. Lambeth Palace—I cannot stop to tell anything about it that you ought to know; only I read in his own handwriting that curious sentence,

"Dum spiro, spero. Charles R.,"

of the poor king who lost his head. How I wondered when and moved by what impulse he wrote it! And a story told by the custodian as we passed an empty niche which had once contained the statue of Thomas a Becket: Some repairs were being made. It was remarked by one of the workmen: "That niche once held a saint; now the niche remains, but the saint is gone." Immediately another spoke up: "Did he leave his address?"

We gave the good part of a day to Whitehall afterwards, and saw the spot where Charles was beheaded, and looked through the window of the banqueting-hall, now a chapel, which he walked out of on his way to the scaffold. "Nothing in his life became him like the leaving it."

The Government Buildings, too, proved absorbingly interesting, especially as getting to see them is a privilege. An English cousin is an official, fortunately for us. I saw Gladstone's seat in the Cabinet chamber. And Salisbury's, too, removed to the opposite side of the table. I did not care so much for it. And from there to Temple Bar; the church first, which I had seen several times. Also the dining-hall of the barristers. A member of that honorable body was of our party, a friend of my cousin, and a cousin of the sculptor Flaxman. He is a bachelor and "lives in chambers." As often as I have read that expression, I never thought of trying to realize what it meant. Imagine my excitement and delight when he insisted on our going with him to his chambers for "five o'clock tea." It was raining, dismal and chilly outside. Such a lot of crazy, queer, enchanting little cuddy-holes as we were ushered into! I'll tell you all about them by and by. He saw my fascinated gaze at an old clock, and at once invited me to a prowl with him. I don't know how many little dens he took me into, each stuffed full as they could hold of antique gems, curios, etc.; among them several lovely old clocks, aged three hundred years and more. The conclusion of our prowl was the crowning delight: *he gave me one!* I don't know what I said, but I know he will live forever in my heart. He was a charming host, and I hope he will invite us again!

Next, we spent two days at Canterbury, not only "doing" the cathedral, but rambling about the quaint and curious old town, and getting impressions of its inhabitants, so unlike ourselves. We attended vesper services in "Little St. Martin's on the Hill," where Christianity was first preached in Great Britain by St. Augustine. Some parts of its walls are 1,500 years old. I am not going to make a guide-book of my letter, but if you don't know about this church it is worth your while "to read up" on it. Then we crossed the channel, and brought up at Amiens. Its cathedral and museum are temptations to all tourists. We loitered two days before coming here. The time was well put in. I fear I am more humane than esthetic though, for I was more interested in an institution, quite modern and altogether practical, into which we stumbled, as it were. It was for children whose mothers were out doing work by the day. They are clothed, fed and educated, as well as kept from morning till night. I had read about such an institution years ago in a book by Sir Francis Head, called "A Faggot of French Sticks."

And here — well Paris *is Paris!* The weather interferes though. It is rain, or clouds, or fog, or dampness, almost all the time. Sight-seeing does not prosper under such auspices. Still we have seen a great deal. Among those that have fastened on my memory, like tar on one's best gown, is "a sight I saw" at the Jardin des Plantes. In one of the cages of the wildest of the wild beasts a dog and tigress are dwelling, and have dwelt together in peace and harmony for six years! And the birds and the animals seemed as conscious of observation and as eager to excite admiration as their kindred, the human race. There is nothing more interesting here, I think, than this garden. The collection and arrangement of the plants are something wonderful. Then its age, 250 years, and the association of great names, such as Cuvier, Buffon, Humboldt, etc., give a vivid impression of the value of men to mankind.

I have had some new experiences in various ways. Several trips on the Seine in long, slender steamers called swallows, both by day and night, moonlight and gaslight. And drives on the quais, the most magnificent I know of. Palaces and palaces, and gardens and gardens, on the one hand, and the grand balustrade overhanging the river, with its myriad crafts, all repeated on the opposite bank, the drive bordered by double rows of trees. One can't help owning the beauty, grandeur and completeness of this Paris, not all of it like that of youth "La Beaute du Diable." I have met some pleasant people, too. And was at a Thanksgiving Dinner, turkey and mince pies, American fashion. Everything tempting, but the pies looked so delicious, I said to myself as the hostess was cutting them, "If she does not give me a big piece, I shall wish I had not come." She did!

L. G. C.

Paris, December 6, 1885.

PARIS.

MY return will be delayed a few weeks longer. It was a trial to feel I must submit to this at first, but since these dreadful storms have been raging on the ocean and coasts I have become reconciled. I have had my share of "old ocean's buffetings."

I am here en route for home. Miss B—— came from Sweden to Berlin and remained there a week. She had never been there before. Then she came here, to join the lady with whom she had crossed and was to recross. On reaching here, our program had to be changed. The Arizona was not to sail at the appointed time, being postponed to meet the new postal arrangements. Miss B——'s friend got her head set on the Nile trip. Miss B—— was all eagerness. They would not go without me. The position was embarrassing. So I had to consent. We leave day after to-morrow. Think of it! You have bantered me to write to you from Europe, Asia, Africa, and so on! Perhaps you will get a line or so from under old Cheop's unfathomable countenance, or from melodious Memnon's colossal knee. How I wish he—it—would burst forth once more into that mournful plaint, just for me!

L. G. C.

Paris, December 3, 1886.

PARIS.

YOURS of the 23d February came last night. I had spent the evening out. It was pleasant, indeed, to find letters and papers on my table awaiting me.

Sorry I disappointed you about the Jerusalem trip. "It was not my fault," you may be sure. That is one of the drawbacks of traveling in a party. The composing members are much given to pulling different ways and not making any sacrifice of individual preferences. This friction is trying, but the "kindly race of men" (Heaven save the mark!) is gregarious, and traveling alone is almost worse. So— o— o—h! Next time you shall have a letter written in the shadow of the temple; perhaps another under a canopy of the boughs of the Cedars of Lebanon; and yet another within sound of the purling brook of Hebron. Be consoled. Above all, do not doubt that I shall make contributions from every "grand division" to your entertainment. It is not so long ago you prodded me with that expectation on your part.

Not that I missed its flavor of mockery, *ma foi!* Ah! the "golden fair enchanted" future, that holds the goals of all our ambitions, the realities of all our dreams, the crowns of all our victories!

Do not send the book. Anxious and eager as I am to see it, I am not willing to run the risk of missing it. I am no nearer a decision as to the date of sailing than this: it will not be earlier than the 26th of this, or later than the middle of next, month. If the latter, because I will have waited for company. Some very agreeable ladies are going then, and have urged me to wait. When I persisted in holding the negative attitude, one became exasperated and burst forth, "I bet five dollars you will." Didn't "Old Kaintuck" speak out then? And if I must tell on myself, I have not felt so sure I would not since!

I like the title of the book more and more. There is genius in it. Whose? Don't tell me not yours. It is "so smart," as they say in Kentucky. I never think of it without its stirring my brain to try "to think up" a better one. It must be "a brilliant success."

We are in a tremendous hubbub. "Madame" is "moving." We are going to be almost "next-door neighbors" to Queen Isabella.

As soon as in order, "Madame" gives a house-warming. She is a generous soul, and ought to be a *chatelaine.* Her grandmother was a duchess at the court of Louis XVI. She never not only omits them, but makes chances to give entertainments. An invalid heiress follows with "a five o'clock tea" in her private salon. There will be rivalry of *tea-gowns;* mine is ready. Ever since I gave it a trial donning on its coming from "the man-tailor," they have called me "Lady Collins." Bloom and beauty having departed, age and wrinkles are — knighted. Heigh, ho! why could not one have all honors together?

L. G. C.

Paris, March 8, 1887.

PARIS.

HERE I am still. You will doubtless be surprised. I am.

Day after to-morrow will be a birthday anniversary, and everybody has found it out! Ugh! Think what a nightmare the prospect of that tell-tale cake, with its little wax tapers to the number of my years!

You don't know about the cake. My dear good landlady *will* observe the birthdays of her guests with a grand dinner. This cake is the "grand pièce de résistance," borne into the room and making the circuit of the table with its little tapers, for the inspection of everybody. Would you like such a fireworks' display of your years?

Well, being a man, maybe you would not care. But do not pronounce on me. Just wait till you are transmigrated into a woman to come into a knowledge of our much abused reserve on this point.

If a woman ever is "the weaker vessel," believe me just here is where it comes in. The idea of home dominates her, though the home itself has been desolated and broken up forever. This is not all in my case.

Do you know what it is to have dispensations of conscientiousness? I am sorely troubled at times, and the trouble grows. It seems such a life of idleness and self-gratification this I am living, one of luxurious wandering and enjoyment of the fair face of this lovely mother earth, and beautiful accumulations from all times and nations and peoples. The flight of time—Schiller says—

> "Arrowy swift the present fleeth."

But to me the years now seem come and gone like lightning flashes.

Shall I tell you how the days go? Will you care to hear? It cannot be but that much of interest should come into them. The "sight-seeing," of course, never comes to an end. Think how impossible when I tell you the "Salon," just opened for its annual exposition, numbers largely over 5,000 works; thirty-seven rooms of pictures! I spent yesterday afternoon in them. Guess the wear on eyes, feet and brain of the most cursory survey. At last I had to sit down, and close my eyes to shut them all out, *if* I could. As if I could!

Why I could not even sleep for their haunting, though I went to bed before ten to spare my eyes from further seeing. One gorgeous "Cleopatra," Cabanal's, proved as irresistible a sorceress to me as if I had been a Caesar or an Anthony. It represents that incident given by Plutarch in his "Life of Anthony," when, after the battle of Actium, dreading what may happen to herself, she is having deadly poisons tried on prisoners condemned to death, to find out which would cause the least suffering. I shall not go into a description, but, if possible, will get a photograph, and show you that to give you some idea. Another historical incident, from the brush of Charrier, is that of the Empress Ariadne, who, becoming disgusted with the excesses and cruelties of her husband, the Emperor Zeno, had him, when he was—some say in an epileptic fit, others drunk—walled up in the royal tomb. She is standing beside it, bending in the attitude of listening to his furious struggle. Such a picture has a dreadful fascination. Another, by Constant, is of "Theodora," throned in all her oriental barbaric magnificence. This is Sara Bernhardt's great character, and the picture is very like her, whether or not meant for a portrait.

I saw her in it. Do not think I am going to surfeit you on pictures though.

Here is something about living, working, worth-having-been-born women. Two French *ladies* of the St. Germain exclusive strain. Parents gone, fortune gone, health gone for years. Then the struggle for a living. You can't think how interesting I find them. One is a genius, an exquisite musician, a composer. Some of her compositions are the daintiest, most poetical and pathetic I ever listened to. She is a writer of books as well, charming ones at that. The other is a singer. They gave me a Musicale a few nights ago. I saw some most entertaining messieurs. One in particular, could not speak English, but could read it. You should have heard him discuss Scott, Dickens, and Shakespeare; the last with a fervid enthusiasm. I'll tell you more of these "anon." One beautiful, *fellow* countrywoman, "divinely tall and most divinely fair," proves delightful. She invites me to "four o'clock tea and home-made cake," and what talks we have, and what bouts of sauce, not to say wit!

Then Paris is looking its loveliest in the witchery of May greenness and bluest of skies that fairly laugh. Long walks and longer drives and dawdles, and *prowls* in which plethoric purses are swiftly *depleted.* I can not keep a sou in my pocket. How much I shall have to tell, but I know who will never — listen!

L. G. C.

Paris, April 20, 1887.

PARIS.

AH! you good friend, both the letter and the book have come. If either had come by itself, I would have thanked you most for it; but as they came together, I—I thank you most for — both. How could I do less? "Fifty-two, did you say it was?" No, I did not say. I never meddle with figures. If I do, I am sure to get the worst of it. I do not like to get worsted. Do you? As for a woman's telling her age, who expects it? The silly! As a matter of fact, I can say, in a general way, I am old enough, though I might be older; and young enough, though I might be younger. I might be sixty-two; I might be even no more than forty, yet the trouble is I am neither. So far as all the world is concerned, it has no concern whatever in the matter. So far as you are, I have a misgiving you know without my telling. I only wish you had not known before you finished the book; and that you had asked me, and when I thus declined to tell on myself, you had wrought yourself into a fume about it. But don't I feel cheated that I shall never know how you would have threshed out that cereal! Is not it a curious fact that overproduction is one of the ills of the present period of our little planet's history?

Those thousands of pictures! That magnificent, enormous "Salon!" Can you believe it—there are ever so many other "Expositions" in full blast? They come in such numbers and swift succession, to see each is to wipe out the memory of the one just seen as the succeeding wave does that just gone before. Yet the great names are a temptation you do not even dream of struggling against. You would not if you could. The last time it was Millet's. I hope you have seen his "L'Angelus," or at least an engraving. There is the original or a replica, in Baltimore, I think, which has been exhibited in the United States. I had seen an engraving only, but it was an imperishable memory. When it was mentioned as one of a full collection of his works to be exhibited, you will see I could not have missed it.

I wish I dare attempt to describe the many out of it that won at once my most enthusiastic homage. Almost all peasants and peasant life, shepherds and shepherdesses, with their flocks, peasant women feeding children or chickens, harvest fields and gleaners—the subjects so simple and homely, the treatment just the magic of brush and colors, the mastery of genius. Not all held me equally; but all that I liked held me absolutely. I never had a more unalloyed enjoyment. How I wish I could buy all of them and bring them home with me! Not one was for sale, all being loaned by their owners for the purpose of realizing enough to erect a monument to his memory.

But I can't talk any more about pictures. I want to thank you for "the little book." Thank you for it, from its very inscription, through every phase of its working out, to the finished volume I have just read and laid down with a pang because it is ended, because there is no more. *It is a book.* It is worth having written; worth having taken time to write. It merits all the praise lavished upon it. There is not a word too much. It may be like all those they liken it to, but it is most like yourself. There can be no question of the brilliancy within, the handling of such vast and varied materials; of the enormous reading, the close attention, the critical observations, the careful judgment, the good taste, necessary for such an acquisition of knowledge and information as you have so delightfully utilized. The best about it is not that it is brimming over with this information, brilliancy, entertainingness, power, but that it is full of wisdom as well. The combination to such degree is not common.

It came—"the little book"—at nine last night. I read the letter, and another from another gentleman, then began to handle *it*. I cut the string; took off the wrapping; looked at the binding; pondered over the title, liking it better and better; then—the reluctant plunge. I knew I ought not begin reading, as if I should become interested I could not stop. Late reading tells so on me. Besides, it is the worst form of "late"—keeping right on till the book is finished. Well, you or some one had cut only a part of the leaves. You got the full credit. I said when I began: "How thoughtful in him to cut the leaves." Directly I found some were left for me to do—of course, exactly when I could least bear to lose a moment. My paper-knife went through with a rip, I can tell you. On again, almost holding my breath, or swept away in a convulsion of laughter. Then more leaves to cut. I became suspicious, and said something not altogether amiable, maybe: "He did this on purpose." There was repetition of cut and uncut all the way through; and I shall always believe, even though you convince me to the contrary, that you did this with malice prepense—knowing the obstruction and interruption would act like salt on thirst. At midnight I said: "I will not read another word." I was very tired, having had a long drive, nearly from noon till night. A word about that drive. It was with an invalid heiress, the same I have mentioned. I wish she and you might "make a match of it." She is so bright and every way agreeable, besides having the fortune!

The drive was in the Champs Elysées and the Bois du Boulogne, the fashionable resort. It is always a kind of gay carnival of fashion. The brilliant afternoons; the handsome equipages, the elegant occupants arrayed as not Solomon in all his glory was. The—your—sex not less so than mine! You ought to have seen one I saw yesterday. Alone in his open carriage, evidently "got up" to attract attention; a lilac ribbon tie; vest of silk, matching in color; boutonnière of flowers in the same dainty color; and pantaloons of plaid lilac and white. Was not that a spectacle? But once in the beautiful park, such visions were lost sight of. The sky, air foliage and flowers were Eden's own. I got out of the carriage and gathered *her* hands full of daisies and anemones. She sat in the shadow and quiet of the trees watching me. One avenue was specially interesting. On the left were pretty bits of water, scarcely lakes, low hills with tumbling cascades, stretches of thick-set trees and flowery hedges. On the right, vanishing distances of the greenest sward, edged with scattered clumps of trees, blotched with alternate sunshine and shadow. Away off rose the hills that encircle Paris—a misty greenish-black rampart against the sky. Sometimes we talked; sometimes were silent. These blessed long days! At six o'clock we came home, lest she should become too much fatigued. But I could not stay indoors, and went out again for a walk. I came back loaded with old-fashioned spice pinks—have not you some in your garden?—and great golden marguerites.

But "the little book." This morning I was at it again long before getting-up time. The maid smiled when she came in at seven. And now I have read it, and knowing the pleasure of the reading, I can not help wishing more of it was still to do.

Hurry and write another, please. Why not

"A Club of Two. From the note-book of a woman who *was* sociable?" Beat Mrs. Caudle if you like, or Prue. I am so glad you have given "Prue and I" a place in your book. It has always been one of my giving-away books. Only the other day I was telling of it to some who do not know it. Think of their loss.

Can not say a word about coming, but that it will be soon.

L. G. C.

Paris, May 29, 1887.

VENICE.

YOURS of May 17th "just to hand." Date of your previous one, April 23d—I mean its receipt. This is what I call a most unreasonable space to let slip between. So you see, if the letters come oftener, I complain (being conscience-stricken, thinking I am imposing on your good-nature), and if they lag a little, I complain of that. If you can, match me with a more telling illustration of the impossibility of satisfying a woman! I am writing with some qualms, I can tell you. You did not ask me to write till I got to Switzerland. A mighty neat way of putting the spaces in for me as well as yourself! Did you ever make a note of that distich of John Hay's—

"There be three things which when you think they are coming are going—
When you think they are going are coming—
A crawfish, a diplomat and a woman?"

I could not get it in right, but that will not hinder you from taking in that I am like to go

The Old Lion at the Arsenal, Venice.

contrariwise. Besides, I know what you will miss if I do not write—enough to make you go into mourning, a bit of crape at your buttonhole. You don't know what a Florence letter I wrote to you! Now, I am not given to self-praise; but I know the difference between still and sparkling catawba, glass and diamonds—stupidity and sparkle.

So I speak, "having authority"—that Florence letter, written to you long before I was up or the sun either; yes, just as Guercino's maidens, fashioned of dusk and dawn, were beginning to put the stars out—that was a letter! Had it only have reached you, *it* would have thrown you into a fit of St. Vitus' dance, or something equally demonstrative. I am a light sleeper, late to bed, later to sleep and early awake. I cannot get up ahead of all households, so I do not even hold in the fitful fancies, but let them have it all their own way. Such fascination as the habit is! I just snap my fingers at the frowning brows of Messrs. Abercrombie, Upham, Sir William Hamilton and all that cloud of accordant authorities on mental discipline. And for that letter, as for me, I did not have any more to do with its flash and fun and sauce and sparkle than one who sits on the sea-shore and watches the waves in a frolic, or as Longfellow says it for me:

> "—— sits in revery and muses
> Upon the changing colors of the waves that break
> Upon the idle seashore of the mind."

Ah! if you had only got that letter! Alas! and alas! it was never even put on paper. You do not know how sorry I am, though, that you can never, never see it, and read it, and pirouette over it, and maybe frame it and hang it up on your walls, to be a memorial of me forever and forever. Indeed, I did so want you to have a Florence letter, for you know somebody, Rogers maybe, says:

> "Of all the fairest cities of the earth,
> None is so fair as Florence.
> —— Search within,
> Without; all is enchantment!"

It was so while I was there! The forenoons with Raphael, Angelo, Fra Angelica, Carlo Dolce, Guercino and a few others; the afternoons in long drives among the haunts of Galileo, Mrs. Browning, Landor, and such spirits. Will you ever know the delight of it, the beatitude? I hope so. Don't put off the coming till you are too old. But now I am in

VENICE.

Venice! In Venice in June! And yesterday and to-day have been each the very one described as I have read somewhere: "The day was one of those which can come to the world only in early June at Venice. The heaven was without a cloud, but a blue haze made mystery of the horizon where the lagoon and sky meet. The breath of the sea bathed in freshness the city, at whose feet her tides sparkled and slept." And to-morrow will be the same; and day after day I feel in all the spirit of a prophetess. Indeed, the weather might have been blown from Paradise. Drifting about in a gondola! The largest, most ecstatic breath you ever drew must come in right here. Even that will not express the exquisite, intangible bliss of such existence. It eludes words as quicksilver eludes the grasp. I am having long mornings, enchanting afternoons, whole days of it. Do you wonder if I feel as if under some magician's spell? Come, take a drift with me, and find out for yourself. First, the length of the Grand Canal. Your gondolier is behind; you do not see him. There is nothing to save you from your enchanted fate. The blue sky above; the crystal waves beneath; the beautiful, stately old palaces on either side, time-stained, unlike anything you ever saw, a fascination to sight and dreams, that will haunt you the rest of your life; the other gondolas sliding by; now and then a pleasure-boat, with its crowded deck and gay awning, and though moving by steam as noiseless as ours—no smoke; presently another bridge shows its span ahead, and then you slip under it and on; next you are idly noting a pleasant looking party of ladies and cavaliers coming from the cool archway of a palace to their waiting gondola, and you are a little startled by hearing behind the gondolier's voice, "That is where Lord Beeron lived." You remember you had meant to ask him to point out that particular one. You rouse, lean forward, give a curious gaze, then drop back into your drift and dreams, powerless to keep from it! Ah!—that is the Rialto. You rouse again, and give another intense look, and then it is left behind. You shoot another bridge and—you give it up. This can not be earth. You know it is not heaven. Where are you? Surely you are at last on the direct way to it. Heaven—the Heaven of not your reading the Sunday-school and catechisms taught, but of your dearest dreams and purest moods—that is awaiting you there in

Lord Byron's Palace, Venice.

that dazzling glory of silver radiance where the sky and water meet. You lean forward involuntarily, your very soul in your eyes, striving to pierce that shining veil right to the Great Mystery. You do not feel baffled. You might have done it, only the gondola has curved into a side canal and your vision is shut from sight. Best so. One could not bear such ecstasy longer and live, I think. But you are like one in a trance for the rest of the way. Before you sleep, you open your little day-book to make a record of the day. Here is what will greet you when you turn its pages in the future—"Perfect, Perfect Venice." That is all. Will you smile over it then? I wonder. Dear me! I hope not, for the experience has come *after* my head is gray. Earlier you know—

> "Little we dream when life is new,
> And pleasures fresh and fair to view,
> While beats the heart to pleasure true
>   As if for naught it wanted.
> That year by year, ray by ray,
> Romance's sunlight dies away,
> And long before the head is gray,
>   The heart is disenchanted."

No! no! a thousand times, no! You will droop over it and dream it all over again, and thrill and throb with the remembered rapture as even now—

"For passionate remembrance' sake."

You are good to tell me so much of your life. I am glad you had the gracious hours at C—— with your friend. Will his verdict have anything to do with the fate of the "Essays?" But you must never think of me as a judge and critic. I appreciate, enjoy and have a wonderful fund of enthusiasm, once it is set going. As for anything that does not "commend itself to my taste," I simply turn away from it. Why use the scalpel or scathing tongue? I should be marvelously well-pleased, though, to have a reading of the Essays.

I had a letter, so long in the coming, from Miss B—— some days since; so was already in possession of the "pitiful story." No, not that. I think whatever comes to us is our true work, hard as it may seem at the time. Did you ever see or hear of an argument of William Corry's in his prime that had a speech of Caesar's in it? One line of it left its brand in my memory. John (my husband) brought it to me to read when he was George Pugh's partner, and we were living in Cincinnati. "If I am to die to-morrow, then that is what I have to do to-morrow." John declaimed it for me as he had just heard Mr. Corry. It was never to be forgotten. I hope you have written to her ere this is in your hands, and may your words be indeed helpful, inspiring. How often we all need such. She is a splendid creature, so gifted for a household deity! "Caterer, cook and nurse," who so shines at the festal board, in the fireside circle, wherever knowledge, wit and wisdom shed their light and graces! All that is wanting is the proper sphere. And yet there be those so blind they will not see! *Who* is of them?

What have you found in me that gave you leave to think I cared specially for "Kentucky gossip," or indeed for any gossip? Please, if you have such an impression, seek for a revised edition of me. "Assuredly" (Mahomet's cuss-word), your letters hitherto have not run to gossip and I have not complained. "A continuation of the same to the same," may chance to be all sufficient.

Yes, do not hunt up strange fiddle-strings on my account. You know I have reached the years where old strains are best. "All the same," write whatever goads you to bestow it upon me. Oh! I glanced from my window— if you could just see that overarching sky, that *is* heaven; if you could drink in a draught of this air, that is very elixir of life, if—if you could see what I see, feel what I feel. Oh! oh! oh! Perfect, perfect Venice!

L. G. C.

Venice, June 8, 1883.

LUCERNE.

SATURDAY, at Zurich, yours of June 26th "came to hand." Here in the filtered waters of glacier torrents, I drink to the letters that are never written! Now for your response. Let it be brilliant as the dewdrops of early morning, alluring as was to our childhood that trip to find the end of the rainbow with its reward of a bag of gold, satisfying as his day to Longfellow's "Blacksmith."

"Something attempted, something done." Be sure it be of many simples "composed in all parts to perfection." See to it you fall not short of Lamb's happy hit—only this and nothing less.

Are you ready? I am in Switzerland. Bow your head; here is a snow-cap. Crane your neck; here is a chain of the Rigi's lightning. Now straighten to your loftiest stature; only that can wear this mantle of clouds I snatch from the shoulders of Pilatus to fling over yours. And last, here is a dazzle of sunlight to set you in—like a saint in an aureole.

How do you feel? Do not be frightened. You are not ready for your apotheosis; and I am no high priestess. Besides, in a breath you will seem to yourself never to have been other than the grand creature I have made you. You know that vital quality of us mortals that makes us feel we are greater than anything that comes to us.

"We feel that we are greater than we know."

Just to think my last letter was from Venice. How long ago that seems, eons and eons! "I have lived so much since then." Can I ever tell you the half? Ah! me! No, no. Only this impotent—I wish, oh! how I wish I could!

I have ransacked "ancient Padua," thinking of exiled Romeo. Saw the great wooden horse of Danatello, that stands in the largest hall in Europe; holds sixteen men and is taken to pieces, carried down into the street, and put together again and used in procession on fête occasions. "Think of that Master Brook!" It is really a splendid, spirited-looking creature. Did any of your traveled friends ever tell you about it? I saw also, besides "the thousand things" I must omit, Goethe's palm tree, the one he made use of in his theory of the Metamorphoses of Plants. The tree remains and flourishes. The man—where is he? "Light, give us more light," were his last words. I think he has found it. From Padua, I hastened to Verona. Such a beautiful old city! There I sought out Juliet's tomb, in the old monastery hid away in its garden. And I found the house of the Capulets, and stood in its court and gazed with eager interest at that queer hat carved on its shield, placed above the entrance in the wall. This repeated itself on columns and in different places, giving evidence of the prominent position of the family. I was quite unprepared to find the situation of Verona so picturesque, and one feature I have not seen elsewhere, that of its innumerable mills on wheels to be run into and out of "the rapid Adige." Just fancy a line of these queer-looking structures some distance from shore, working away with all the impetuosity that swift current can give, and as steadily as is their wont! But everything about that Shakespeare-famed city is unique and fascinating. Thence to Milan, where I lingered a week, but was not specially impressed. The Cathedral is all that descriptions and pictures make it, and the Milanese claim for it, "the eighth wonder of the world." I climbed to its tip-top perch, and every step revealed some marvel of architecture and sculpture. The workmanship is amazing. You have read all about it, and doubtless think you have a very good idea of it; but just come and stand before it and haunt it, and you will despair of ever taking in the half of its details! No two ornaments or points are alike! I quickly gave up, and looked away from it to the everlasting hills, too far away to force me to mathematical calculations. Have you read of the Grand Victor Emanuel Gallery, that "finest arcade in the world," in shape like a cross, with an octagon center surmounted by a dome, and paved with beautiful mosaic, where the finest shops are, and which is the fashionable promenade, lit by 2,000 gas-lights, and—goodness! if I go on, you will think I am preparing to rival Badeker and get up a guide-book. Well, I just want you to know my apartments were on it, and I was quartered equal to a queen! Everything was gold and glitter, and grandeur and gorgeousness. And I took to it as naturally as a lark to the highest regions of air! Of course, I saw all the libraries, picture galleries, strange old churches, etc., and drove at the fashionable hour on the Corso, watching the gay and festive throngs in carriages, on horseback and afoot, this last most characteristic feature, perhaps, of all I saw. The fair dames in superb toilets holding levées in their splendid equipages! I enjoyed the spectacle. Then I sped away to the Italian lakes. Guess how my heart beat at the prospect of seeing those romantic sheets of water. That was a summerland, indeed, with tideless summer seas and tropical blooms and sounds and sights! Nightingales sang there night and *day*. Magnolias, oleanders, mimosas and myrtles were in full bloom, and the sun shone with almost pitiless fervor. I saw them all in their length and breadth. I haunted their shores and floated over their lovely green waters. And I fell in love with that bijou, Lake Lugano. Next to our own Lake George, it is the most exquisite sheet of water I have ever seen, and I have seen so many!

Presently, almost before I knew, it was "time to move on." That is a hardship sometimes. But it was Switzerland that was awaiting me, and a brand-new experience. You know how it must have been—the heart-breaking at the leaving, and yet springing forward with a bound of eagerness to the unknown. You must have experienced that mixed feeling!

What have I not seen and felt in this wonderland! Unspeakable Switzerland! Every place has its own special exceeding beauty or grandeur, or both. I came into it from Chiavenna, by the Val Bregaglia and Maloja Pass, my first halt being at San Moritz, in the Upper Engadine. This is a fashionable watering-place, in the midst of the most glorious mountain and lake scenery, and is a good point from which to make excursions. I think I shall only tell you of the one I am the proudest of. It was my grand climb. First, a drive of seventeen miles to the Bernina Hospice, among the Bernina Alps, and from there a walk of two and a quarter hours, up, up, to heights far above the tree line, into the vast solitudes of barren rock and eternal snows—7,800 feet high. Behold me, with alpenstock, giving all my energy and enthusiasm to it; sometimes by pretty lakes and prettier tarns—"those wee lakes that looked like tears dropped in the clefts of lofty mountains;" over bridges spanning turbulent streams; across narrow ledges of rock and snow; up cliffs that made me wish I was a kid or a chamois; and ever upward, till my breath was mere gasping! At last I was there, at the Sassal Massone, perched on a shelf in the mountain-side, looking on such a spectacle as I may never see again—the Palu Glacier, sweeping down between two immense mountains, on my right; opposite, mountains; to the left, a lovely valley, clothed in the richest, tenderest verdure, and holding an exquisite lake in its bosom. I gazed and shut my eyes, and gazed and shut them again and again. This Sassal Massone is a little refreshment-house cut into the solid rock on a shelf or terrace, with a seat for the weary climber to rest on while taking in the sublime views.

Thus sitting, a chance turn of my head showed rows of the edelweiss, that lovely, downy, little Alpine flower, just back and a little above me, growing right out of the snow. I sprang up to look at them, and then went to the keeper of the rude hostelry to buy some. He said they were not for sale; that he kept them for tourists to see; but that he would provide me a guide to take me to great fields of them not so very far away. The guide came—the most loutish, stupid-looking creature a mission ever was intrusted to. We tramped through the snow, kept to our feet by our alpenstocks and to the goal by our excitement. It was indeed a vast field of snow, unbroken but by the quantities of the curious little flowers, which seemed cut out of felt—white, but not snow-white; just the tinge of common felt. The petals radiated from a pretty center, a cluster of delicate, palish-gold-colored flowers. The guide looked from them to us and from us to them, then smiled, stepped back and bowed—awkwardly, to be sure—for us to pluck for ourselves. He was instantaneously transformed from the stolid clodhopper I had thought him to be—not to a god, but a mortal with a beautiful soul.

I gathered to my heart's content—all that I could carry on the return tramp. If only I could have brought away the mountain-side with them! The mere thought made me gasp. With hands full and head and heart fuller, full to their utmost, I turned away and "came down from the mountains." I saw three grand glaciers that day; walked to the foot of one, and stood gazing in fascination on its fissured walls of ice and its dangerously beautiful grotto, from which "a glacier torrent" was pouring forth. Everywhere, except at the very highest points, multitudes of the loveliest wild flowers were blooming! Is not that a day to be set apart in one's life? I am sure I shall never recall it without feeling myself a grander creature.

From San Moritz to Thusis by the Julier and Schyn Passes. All the routes have been planned to take in the finest if not most familiarly known scenery. These passes were another experience of the most varied wildness, grandeur, bareness and loveliness. First, the slow zigzag of the diligence into the bleakest regions of grey cloven rocks, piled into "Alps upon Alps," till they towered far up above the snow line; then great tortuous windings down into the heart of such luxuriant vegetation as is not surpassed, hardly equaled, by that of Ohio's fertile valleys and hills. Then—I would lend you my eyes if I could, just to have you realize what a panorama of sublime beauty Switzerland can give, but I have no words to picture it. Thusis is situated at the entrance of the Via Mala, the famous gorge through which that impetuous stripling, the young Rhine, rushes with such headlong recklessness. A wide and long-extended valley, surrounded by every kind of mountain and height, from knolls to snow peaks; two rivers tearing in at one end, uniting and hurrying onward as the Rhine right through the center, and twenty towns dotting the distances, with castles and churches perched in every romantic spot. Why, it seemed to me the earth was growing more beautiful and wonderful every moment.

The ruins of the oldest castle in Switzerland, on the summit of a spur of the Muttnerhorn, a lofty, rounded mass of rock, partly covered with trees and grass and flowers, partly showing only sheer rifts of limestone, rose just in front of my windows. I sat on my balcony and saw the moon rise among its crumbling towers sail slowly across and above them, and mount to the highest heavens; while below me a fine band played such music as was in perfect harmony with that enchanting spectacle and my own mood. Next forenoon I drove the length of the Via Mala, and on my return left the carriage and climbed to that seductive height all alone, my companion begging off. No, not quite alone. I had some goats and kids for companions, and am gregarious enough to own I was glad of even them. They just looked at me with a mild curiosity, and nibbled on or clambered ahead or waited to let me pass. Perhaps—who knows?—a biped innovation was as pleasant to them as they were to her! The view at the top was all I thought it could be. And that is my description in full. Is it not satisfactory?

There is a legend about this ruin that haunts

me. The last lord of the castle blindfolded his horse and leaped from that fearful height to certain and awful death. I have seen since I was there a picture by one of Switzerland's first artists representing this scene. No danger of my ever forgetting it now. Then I sped along that rampageous youngster's course for several hours, all aglow over the wonders it unrolled before me, till nightfall brought me to Ragatz, another fashionable watering-place. Its environs possess, in addition to all I have heretofore enumerated in the way of mountains, water and vale, what is said to be the most curious and unique feature in this remarkable little commonwealth: a gorge in which hot springs are inclosed. Having seen it, I would not have missed it "for anything," as my French teacher used to say. Imagine an enormous fissure in a vast limestone ridge, a mountain; it might have been cloven there by Atlas in that forepast when such giants were no fiction. The depth must be from 150 to 200 feet; maybe more. Those awe-inspiring walls seem almost to meet; for overhead they swerve in many places toward each other, so as to shut out the light; in others they part to admit gleams of sunshine and blue sky. Far below, a glacier stream, the Tamina, is rushing, roaring, throwing up clouds of spray, and wearing away now, as it has been wearing away for lo! how many thousand years, that *not* too solid rock.

A wooden gallery runs along one side following the sinuosities of the rock, and you have a walk of a quarter of a mile through this strange, weird, yes, appalling "work of nature," wrought by that foaming torrent, to the vaulted passage, "dark as Erebus," which leads to the springs. Niagara is not grander or more imposing than this Plutonian gorge in its way. But, dear me, I will never get through if I try to tell you a tithe of what I have done and seen. For you see, there is the ascent of Rigi and ever so much else. Well, "the play will have to be cut." I went up Rigi in the cars, saw a sublime sunrise, and walked down on the other side to Küssnacht! Believe me, I will never do the like again. It was a four-hours' tramp, or rather slip and slide, stumble, stick, stagger. The way is always steep, and then it was slippery from the recent rains. I am just getting over the stiffness and soreness. No, I would not do it again for Rigi itself. But this Lucerne is just perfect loveliness, and I am getting "restored" rapidly.

And here I am ashamed of this long letter,

afraid of another sheet, and have not said what I most wish to say. It is about your book. I am sure I shall like it, and hope you will stay at home and get it ready for the public, especially me. Yes, the title is good. I wish I was reading it this moment in print. I hope you have written to Miss B——. Were you at the wedding of Miss S——? Tell me about it. But I must stop. I do not want to —. Good-bye.
L. G. C.

Lucerne, July 26, 1883.

VIENNA.

I SHALL make a beginning, but have no idea when I shall reach the finis. But I thank you beforehand not to say, "and the longest yet," if it should be. All equipped and waiting for the opera hour in Vienna; a pale sunlight dropping from "a lambent sky;" windows wide open,

> "To let the outdoor gospels in;"

an easy enough picture to make to the mind's eye, if you are so "minded." The opera hour is 6 o'clock. Isn't that primitive for the "second Paris," as this metropolis is fondly called by many? It strikes me it is absurdly so and *bien incommode,* as the French say. You see, dinner is the midday meal all over Germany. This places the supper hour at 7.30 or 8. So one has to eat too often or not often enough; "something" before going and a hearty supper afterwards, or only the latter, at 10 or 11. I do not like either way, but generally omit the first; and then!

VIENNA.

Your letter was waiting for me here on Saturday. This is Wednesday. I was "ever so glad" to get it. The one pleasure you can never know in its supremacy till you are "a bronzed wanderer in a foreign land," is that of getting letters. I wish—how I wish!—everybody was as good a correspondent as I am. No matter how often, how brilliant or *how long* their letters were, they would be "more than welcome," as the happy father said on No. 12's advent in the family circle. That is the right spirit, even for a letter. But some people—hm! I can't express them.

Did you mean it? did you know it? your letter was so full of wise suggestions I put on my study-cap, "and Frank Hazeldean sat down to think." To be sure, I *am* doing a great deal—*all* I can. If I do not now, I never shall. I did not make much out of the "brown study" beyond that; and this. If I were Goethe, or any one that was going to be anybody, I would do as thoroughly as he. But to think at my age of going to the heart and bottom of things —how in vain! What is left me but to skim over the surface like a bird over water, now and then dipping in? And anyway, is not a clear, graphic, comprehensive superficiality—I am not sure I can make you understand me—the next best thing to thoroughness? Have you not known people with that gift with whom it was a felicity to be thrown? Felicity may not be—is not—such an ultimatum as beatitude, which is found only in the highest heights and deepest depths; but think of the light, warmth, sparkle, enjoyment, of the middle realms of air? Is that an excuse for my busy idleness? Perhaps. Yet the deeper plunge of my wings comes oftener than you suspect, maybe. The wider knowledge of and the more intimate contact with the works of nature, and no less those of my fellow-men—these have been the gains I have most counted on. My brain "burned with great ideas" equally among the towering ice-peaks and awe-inspiring glaciers of Zermatt, and in the presence of the wrecks of Paestum's sublime temples. To look on such wonders of creation, be the work of divine or human hands, is to be driven inward, far within yourself, in search of the creative motive. If for myself, and my power of accomplishing, I am driven thereby into the depths of "a profound despair," my pride in and homage to the worthier workers are only the greater. But this is enormous egotism. You can have of *me* only what you take. You remember that complaint of Swedenborg to the angel: "I asked you for a fig, and you have given me a grape." "I *gave* you a fig, but you took a grape," was the angel's reply.

I shall try to do your bidding in respect to Paris. I have not meant to do it in haste. Still, neither the lovely city nor "its unknowable, incomprehensible, original" arouse my interest to a very fervid degree. When I have come to know both better, I may change.

18th. Don't you see you are in for a diary? My hostess came in with cake and fruit, plums, pears, peaches and grapes. I must take some before going. Of course Eve listened to the voice of the charmer. She always does, and always with the same result, does n't she?

The opera was one of Wagner's, "Tristian and Isolde." The story belongs to the dim, misty regions of English history, mixed up with Irish in a way quite baffling to one so ignorant of the latter as I am. I wonder if you know the story. Before telling, I shall wait to hear. I may remind you that Wagner as a composer always had an idea or ideas to embody. If you have seen or heard—oh! for a jolt to bring out the right word for witnessing an opera, which is both seen and heard—Tannhäuser, you will catch my meaning. It is a story of temptation, sin and repentance wrought out most powerfully in music of unfortunate love and its penalty. The heroine is a fine-looking woman, and a powerful actress, with a voice equal to Wagner's requirements, which is saying a good deal; but she lacked magnetism! She did not once sweep me into forgetfulness, or impotency of criticism. Interpreting ideas through the highest science of music is a grand and glorious performance, but it is a fearful tax on the human voice. In Dresden, all the singers of his music but one sang as if their voices had been overstrained. Here they sing it as if they had mastered a difficult task, but, like liberty, the price is eternal vigilance. The orchestral music, though, always makes up for other deficiencies. I hardly see how it could be finer or more perfect. The house itself is faultlessly beautiful and comfortable. This last feature is worth making a note of, for the Grand Opera House in Paris is stifling, the most unbreathable atmosphere to which I was ever subjected.

The *mise-en-scene* here and all over Europe leaves nothing to ask for. At home by half-past ten; let in by a concierge, who provided us with a small wax taper to light ourselves up to our apartments. There the post-opera collation was awaiting. Don't you wish you had been one at it? Would not that have been provocation to immense brilliancy? Scintillant as Sirius—that would have been your rôle.

Was it inexplicable that I did not want to get up this morning at all? Yet I had to. Why? I think I have not told you. The object of my pilgrimage here is to have the treatment of the finest aurist in Europe. I am not over-sanguine, but hope for some benefit. Deafness is a very trying deficiency. I dread any increase, so I thought I ought to give myself the chance of even partial "benefit." The custom of "specialists" is to receive the patients at their offices and there treat them. My hour is half-past nine a. m. Hence the loss of that delicious morning dawdle and drowse.

Would you not like a peep into this magician's quarters? They are what may be called "stunning," I can tell you. Every time I go into them I finger my ducats pensively and sigh, "Needless to ask; we know who pays for the piper." First, a square ante-chamber, with frescoed ceiling and pictures on the walls. I have not more than glanced at this. From this two doors, through which I have been passed; one leading to a private reception-room, the other to the public. I go to the former, as I have my hour and am not to be kept waiting. It is an oblong room with green hangings on the walls and very dark, old oak furniture. There is a large cabinet, the glass doors lined with green silk. I have not seen what is in it. In one corner is a beautiful pedestal, on which is a bronze copy of that famous head of Homer in the Naples Museum. Between it and a door leading into the examining office is a Venetian mirror surrounded by small, rare paintings. There is a woman's head that would haunt you for many a day could you see it. There are two handsome glass cases with tier upon tier of the bony structure of the ear mounted beautifully for inspection. In the examination-room, dark, crimson hangings, its ceiling an oval fresco of a blue, summer sky, flecked with fleecy films of clouds; and in the oval border at the ends four medallion portraits of eminent physicians, there is a book-case filled with fine editions of Shakespeare, Byron, Humbolt, Lessing, Goethe, etc., a cabinet of ebony inlaid with ivory, on which stands a bronze

VIENNA. 221

head of Hippocrates, statuettes, curious little clocks, etc. Another cabinet has some dainty bits of china, a pair of candlesticks of tortoise shell inlaid with ivory, and more of such things than would fill several sheets. On the walls are most excellent copies of Rembrandt's portraits of himself and that "wife Saskia" he was so proud of. The frames of these are simply "works of art" in wood carving. Two landscapes by Zimmerman, the first time I have encountered him out of the large and public galleries. The large public reception-room is fit for a palace; the walls from ceiling to floor covered with pictures; tables, cabinets and chairs in ebony inlaid with ivory; rare mirrors and china, etc. Now, I have not enumerated the half. What do you think of it? Is it any wonder I and my ducats have a private confab over it?

From that interview this morning, still not much more than half awake and alert, we went to the Palace to see the "cabinet of coins and antiques." The "coins" always overwhelm me, so much time must be given to do anything with them, so I am disheartened. I passed soon to the "antiques." How your eyes would snap to find themselves gazing at the seal ring of Alaric, a large sapphire with a head in intaglio and a heavy setting looking like hammered gold. What a giant he must have been if the size of the ring did no injustice to the finger. And a large vase of Cleopatra's, gold-gilt with a wide border of exquisite cameos, carvings and precious gems, and the center a portrait of herself in "jewels, rich jewels of the mine." Also, an agate vase of twenty-nine and one-half inches in diameter, from the bridal treasure of Mary of Burgundy. Nothing interested me more than a bronze tablet, with a prohibition of the Bacchanalia, 186 years before Christ. I made out a few words in the time I gave it.

Yesterday morning I was at the Imperial Library, in the same edifice; the right name is the Imperial Berg. There I saw fragments of the Gospel of the Sixth Century on purple parchment with silver and gold letters; of Genesis, of the Fourth; a map of the Roman roads, A. D. 160; Tasso's own copy (manuscript) of "Jerusalem Delivered," and the prayer-book of Charles V. The poet was not sparing of erasures, and the prayer-book was pretty well thumbed. "Men die but their works live after them—" and what tales they do tell on them.

VIENNA. 223

I could write on and on, filling up the interval since the last letter, but, to quote from an old Cincinnati physician, "Enough is a plenty."

L. G. C.

Vienna, October 17, 1883.

SIENA.

FEBRUARY 22d, we took the train for Nice, via Lyons and Marseilles. Spent the first night at the former and remained long enough next morning for a drive that took in the best part of the busy, populous, prosperous city. It is ever so much larger than I was thinking of, and its situation is one of extreme beauty. It is situated at the confluence of the Rhone and the Saone. Those lovely rivers wind picturesquely through it, spanned by handsome bridges—the Rhone by eight and the Saone by thirteen—dividing it into three parts, edged by broad quays and shaded by trees. The ranges of near hills are surmounted by fine residences, from which the loveliest views stretch out to misty mountains in the distance to the east, south and west. Nothing was wanting.

From there to Avignon was simply ravishing. The route descended the valley of the Rhone, almost touching its lapping wavelets. We "stopped off" at Avignon till the next train, which gave several hours—time enough to see the special things I had in my mind. Of course, it was a kind of pilgrimage to the shrine of Petrarch's Laura. We saw the old Papal palace, the home of the popes during that century (from 1309-77) of their residence there. It is an interesting but dirty old pile, being used now as a barracks—French soldiers, in common with their nation, being not especially clean and neat. The torture and the prison towers were interesting historically, but the beautiful faded frescoes on the walls of the popes' private chapel rather obliterated everything else. In one place, Petrarch's face shone forth in almost its original freshness. The hair was golden, and the dark hazel eyes looked straight out with a living look, as if the brain behind were busy over all they looked upon. Mounting a little higher, we peeped into the cathedral; and higher still, we reached the Rocher des Doms, an abrupt eminence laid out in pleasant grounds, that command what is said to be one of the most beautiful prospects in France.

Thence we drove to the Musée Calvet, which contains the Vernet gallery, pictures of the four generations of that family of artists. There was a portrait of Petrarch, over which hung one of Laura. In the garden attached is a simple, tasteful monument to Laura—a square pedestal surmounted by a globe, from which rises a cross with a wreath of flowers hung upon it. It is all of white marble. From there we continued our drive across the bridge, from which is seen an old bridge stretching about two-thirds of the way across the river, with crumbling walls and arches. One end is entirely gone. I am sure it is left just as it is because of its effectiveness as a feature in the view.

Recrossing the bridge, we drove around the greater part of the city to see the fine old walls dating 1349, and still in an admirable state of preservation.

The moon was just full, and rose as we shot out of the station for our sixty-five miles run to Marseilles. We remained at Marseilles for several hours next morning, and had the inevitable drive. It was along the quay, and I had my first glimpse of the "blue Mediterranean." It was an animated and thoroughly foreign spectacle; but the wind was high and biting, and the dust excessive, which made everything and everybody look dirty, even myself; so I was glad to settle down in our car for Nice.

We were soon in the "tropics," olive orchards, orange and lemon groves, almond trees in bloom, palm trees, etc., lining both sides of the track.

At Cannes, an English lady, titled, Lady G——, got into our carriage, and she was thoroughly well-bred and agreeable. The train was crowded, and her husband had to go into another car, our "carriage" being for ladies only. No exception, even for "my lord." Lady G—— then pointed out Gladstone's villa and other beautiful places, and told us with a low, amused ripple of laughter of her gambling at Monte Carlo—it was very mild; she laid down a five-franc-piece, and lost; laid down another, and won; "so I quit even," she said. We went to different hotels. Her carriage and servants in livery were waiting for her; and ours, a special one sent from the hotel for just us two—was waiting for us. Another carriage from our hotel bore thither a handsome baron, with a "love of a dog;" and as we arrived at the same time, our arrival created something of a sensation! It was a lovely hotel, right on the sea front, with a beautiful tropical garden in front—one wing ran out in front too; it was a two-story châlet. I had the corner room with windows taking in all that beautiful out-doors.

I saw the moon rise out of the sea; and at intervals all night, watched her course to her setting. Then I saw the magical clouds and lights of the dawn on the water, and Venus rise and hurry away to herald the sun coming up in all his glory.

We went to hear Bishop Littlejohn, of Rhode Island, at the American Chapel in the forenoon; walked on the fashionable promenade in the early afternoon; then a tram-drive to the cemetery to see Gambetta's monument and grave. The cemetery is on a high hill whose top is a fine plateau. In the most conspicuous part is a large square railed in by an iron fence entirely concealed by floral devices. In the center of this square rises a lofty pyramid, composed of floral offerings of every conceivable device, that were sent, it would seem, from the uttermost parts of the earth, to his funeral. Scattered round are other pyramids of the same. I think they said in Paris there were five hundred thousand floral offerings or tributes sent.

Next day, we made an excursion to Monaco and Monte Carlo! The former has the royal palace atop of a height with a view that would make a lazarone of me! I am sure I could do nothing but sit in "rapt ecstasy" and gaze at the blue sky, through the sycamore branches, or the denser blue sea from the balustrades that run along the edge of the great square in front. There is a barrack also. You know Monaco is one of the smallest kingdoms in the world. Its standing army numbers fifty soldiers! I saw a number of the fine, amiable-looking fellows. They looked trim, immaculate and soldierly, and as if they did not enjoy to the fullest extent their superabundant idleness. I can not attempt to describe the luxurious and sumptuous magnificence of the royal apartments. A lovely drive of ten or twelve minutes took us thence to Monte Carlo. We went into the Casino, the great gambling palace, made the tour of its superb halls and eight large tables crowded with players of both sexes and all ages and ranks. It made me heart-sick in a very few minutes, and I sat apart watching the anomalous and painful spectacle till my companion wearied, too, which was not till she had tried her luck and like Lady G——. "come out even. We had a dream-drive home in the late afternoon. Next morning, a party of seven of us chartered a kind of coach for the celebrated Cornichen drive over the old Roman route as far as Mentone. From there we went to Genoa by train, never out of sight of something of exquisite beauty. Then Genoa for two nights and a day, a "field day" of sightseeing—four palaces, four churches, a drive and shopping! Pisa for another night and day; saw its incomparable group—Duomo, Campanile, Baptistery and Campo Santo. How little I had conceived of their magnificence and beauty! From Pisa to Siena. Such a wonderful old place as this is! We leave to-morrow for Naples, via Rome, for a day, to "do it," and return to Rome for Holy Week and Easter. I set aside three months for Italy, but Rome and Florence are a world in themselves for me. It snowed here yesterday; so it is very cold to-day.

I have had views at intervals of snow-covered mountains from Lyons here. I saw Mont Blanc distinctly—a colossal white specter, towering grandly in the upper heavens—at one point on the way. They said it was about ninety miles distant. They are splendid to look at, but not to feel. This cold on my travels has cut me down so. I am too stupid to write a decent letter.

L. G. C.

Siena, March 4, 1883.

ROME.

I LEFT Paris four weeks ago this morning. I cannot for the life of me remember if I have written to you in that time. Seems to me, though, I wrote from Siena. Anyhow, I will make that my starting point. From there we—the lady who is traveling with me is an Ohioan from G—— originally, and the sister of H. H. B——, the historian of the tribes of the Pacific coast—went to Naples via here. We spent a night and a day driving about in the brilliant sunshine, seeing many points of interest by way of preparation for my return. Then on to Naples. It was raining hard and 11 o'clock at night when we reached it. Several days of promiscuous rain and shine, the former out of all proportion to the latter, rather disgusted me. I could not get to Capri, to Baja, to the top of Vesuvius. I had the views between showers of that world-renowned bay, and went in them to the churches, museums, and the lovely palace, Capodimonte. It both rained and snowed a little while I was inside the last. Of course you know it is atop of one of the loftiest points about N——, and that it is full of pictures and all kinds of lovely things. But there is one painting there I think you may not have heard of—Michael Angelo kissing the hand of his dead friend, Vittoria Colonna. You remember he once afterwards regretted he had not kissed her brow or lips. This is a grand picture, the figures life-size. Vittoria lies shrouded in a rich white satin robe, confined about her feet with laurel branches. The face has a worn look—that of

> "long disquiet
> Merged in rest."

Angelo is bending down, with his lips touching her folded hands and his countenance knotted with grief and the heavy sense of loss. Ah! no future would ever be to him like the past! I felt his loss like my own; and the tears sprang quick and blinding. This was the only picture of them all I brought away with me. At the Museum, the Pompeian frescoes, the Farnese Hercules Bull, made the deepest impression. One of the frescoes, a Nereid on the back of a sea panther, I tried to get a photograph of, but failed. You know Donneker's Ariadne? I think he must have got the idea from this, and as I have it in ivory—the most perfect little gem—I wanted this too. I saw a very curious and interesting spectacle in one of the churches, St. Dominico, in the sacristy: the coffin of the Marchese di Pescara, Vittoria Colonna's husband. It was one of a number, ten of which contained the remains of kings and queens, placed around the walls just below the ceiling. They had faded scarlet covers. On his was an inscription by Aristo; above it, his portrait; at one end, his banner; and attached to the side, his sword. Everything concerning that noble woman is of the deepest interest to me; so I made a pilgrimage to see the portrait and coffin of the lover-husband she has embalmed in her verses.

The rain continuing, we "broke up camp," and went to Pompeii. It poured for a day and a half there; and then the sun burst forth and I spent all Sunday in that exhumed city. Impossible to convey the slightest idea of the fascination of it. Come and try it for yourself. At night Vesuvius added the strange and rather terror-inspiring charm of its glowing crater, slow-flowing lava and brilliant column of smoke rising far aloft. It kept me going to my window all night. I'll tell you about it some day. Next to La Cava, a beautiful town in a vale surrounded by chains of the most picturesque mountain peaks. There it rained and snowed again—snowed heavily on the mountain tops. All the vale was dressed in the "living green" of mid-spring. The snow in it was a March flurry. From there we had a lovely drive—a Cornichean drive—around the headlands of the sea to Amalfi. Read Longfellow's poem "Amalfi." I clambered to the Convent (now a hotel) for the view and lunch. Both were incomparable. Read the poem copied in the Guest-book and shown with great pride, and left as Eve left Paradise, "with reluctant steps and slow." Next day, Paestum! Oh! those inexpressible ruins! What an element *worship* has been in the life of our race. I never realized this more deeply than in those majestic old temples. I gathered *acanthus* from crevices in the crumbling columns and stones of the floors. Next day Castellamare and Sorrento, with another ideal drive between them. At the latter, I went to the finest orange grove in that district, and gathered oranges from the trees for myself. Ah! that was fruit fit for the gods. Naples again and rain. I waited two more days for Capri in vain. Spent them at the Museum, where I fell in love again—

and this time with youth and beauty, a bronze statuette of Narcissus listening to Echo. If I gave myself leave how *I* could *rave* about *it*. I got every photograph I could find and mean to have a copy if I can find one. It was found in Pompeii. What lovers of beauty peopled that ill-fated city.

I have been here since Saturday. Sunday was Palm Sunday at St. Peter's. I went. The grand edifice did not disappoint. The ceremonies and music did. Shall I send you a leaf of the consecrated palm? Monday was spent in getting settled. Tuesday, the Albani Villa. To-day, the Sistine Chapel and Raphael's Transfiguration at the Vatican; and Guido's Aurora at the Rospigliosi Palace.

Have I ever told you how I wished with a passionate intensity to spend a full winter in Rome? and now I am having the fulfillment. Almost I can believe Goethe, "Time brings the fulfilment of what is passionately longed for when we are young." Those are not his words perhaps, but they convey his idea. When I first read them twenty or twenty-five years ago, I did not agree with him. Curious that the flight of time which has made me reject faith in the principle of compensation, should make me a believer in that.

"Whoever," says Chateaubriand, "has nothing else left in life should come to Rome to live; there he will find for society a land which will nourish his reflections, walks which will always tell him something new." Read again what Hawthorne says in "The Marble Faun," that after one has lived in Rome and talked it and left it, he is astonished to find his heartstrings have mysteriously attached themselves to it and are drawing him thitherward again, as if it were more familiar—more intimately his home than even the spot where he was born." Do you know I feel every word of this! If you want to have a touch of this Roman fever read, stopping to make pictures to your mind's eye as you read "The Marble Faun," Hans Andersen's "Improvisatore," Storey's "Robe di Roma," and Ouida's "Ariadne." This last you must give me your opinion of. I have been to all the places she names; almost to all each names. The weather is mild, generally sunshine to make one think the worship of that luminary not the worst the world has ever known.

Spring flowers are thick everywhere. Yesterday brought such a clever letter from

Miss D——. I think I must quote a bit or two to give you " a taste of her quality."

I had sent some Xmas souvenirs to her and her sisters. Of the younger two—very young—she said: "You should have seen D—— and M—— when they told their friends, ' My cousin in Paris sent me this,' with the air of being thankful that they were not as other little girls that had no cousin in Paris."

L. G. C.

Rome, March 19, 1883.

ROME.

WE spent a day at Amalfi. From La Cava, a pretty town in an extensive vale shut in with the most picturesque chains of mountains, we took an open carriage for the three hours' drive. It soon struck the sea-coast and wound all the rest of the way around its headlands, doubling its promontories, retreating into its bays and inlets and dropping almost to the water's edge, and presently mounting upward into almost Alpine heights. The headlands and cliffs were frequently broken into every imaginable form of rock sculpture—columns, cones, pyramids, grottoes and castellated walls of defense and fantastic ruins. The sea beat the shore, here, a sheer precipice, and there a white sanded beach, then rolled away a tangled mass of the most exquisite and innumerable shades of blue, green, purple, black, gold and silver. The coast stretched around in a vast semi-circle of silver till it lost itself in the misty horizon. Little villages lay at our feet, ran up the hill-sides with their terraces of orange-groves, or clung to the cliffs far overhead like martins' nests in winter. A long range of snow-capped mountains reared themselves above Salerno, and sent us an icy blast now and then. There had been quite a snow the day before. We rattled up to our "albergo" at eleven. This was at the foot of the hill; our destination was an old monastery of the Capucins, now a hotel, of which this was the porter's lodge. The same proprietor conducts both. He met us with the welcome accorded to favored guests, and gave us a guide, and we were off at once.

The practical should not be neglected entirely for the picturesque, so, we "took in" on our way, a macaroni factory. We saw the flour, then the kneading, last the moulding. The kneading is quite peculiar, and a long and fatiguing part. There is a flat, round table with a beam that works on and around it, the dough being placed between. Six youths of eighteen or twenty were on the end and worked it up and down and back and forth. The whole had a joint resemblance to a grist-mill and the game of see-sawing. The boys were bare-legged and looked very clean and cool. When the dough is sufficiently kneaded, it is transferred to the mould. This is a cylindrical-shaped machine, filled with the small cylinders through which the dough is forced to convert it into the little tubes with which we are so familiar. The dough is placed on one end and the pressure applied, which forces it through. The several squads of workmen are very eager to show off at their best, their palms tingling, no doubt, in expectation of the accustomed fee.

Leaving this factory, we began climbing steps. The monastery is the hollow of a rock, which rises abruptly from the sea, has cloisters, a veranda, a "terrace-walk," a kind of collonade, and from innumerable points the most charming views. Longfellow had been there ahead of me, for which I "returned thanks" on finding in the guest-book his poem "Amalfi." As I read it my eyes went wandering over all therein so felicitously described. The salon was the refectory of the monks, and each window, glazed to the floor, opened on a veranda. I shut myself out on one, and, leaning on its solid stone balustrade, gave myself up to the dreamy fascination of the "enchanted land." Do read the poem, and try to picture each feature with your mind's eye. The description is perfect. After lingering till the very last moment, we found our guide, and took another route to the albergo, where we had left our carriage.

Whether the descent to Avernus is easy or not depends upon the grade of descent. That was not many degrees removed from "sheer." Believe me, it was not "easy." It dropped us on the beach, and the "white-caps" gave us close chase here and there. Nothing to compare, though, to that of a battalion of little beggars who became so importunate, we had to turn our umbrellas into weapons of both defense and attack, whereupon they yelled and shouted with laughter. So we parted "merry foes," if neither side could boast a triumph.

The earth never saw a more perfect morning than the following. That was to be our Paestum day. Our host, a number of countrymen and countrywomen, even the station porter who carried our lunch basket to a carriage on the train which was to take us part of the way—one and all exclaimed: "How fortunate you are! You could not have a more splendid day to see the ruins." Fourteen miles by rail and then a carriage again for a drive of two and a half hours. The sea was "radiantly beautiful," a wide expanse of flashing wavelets. Leaving it, the route crossed marshy plains, occasionally dotted with small herds of buffaloes and other cattle. The mountains kept along with us, gradually diminishing in height until they sank into the low coast. After awhile the first glimpse of the temples. That was a sensation! It is said of these temples that they were built in the ancient Greek style, and are, with the exception of those at Athens, the finest existing monuments of the kind. The temple of Neptune is the largest and most beautiful of the three. Its magnitude, massiveness and grandeur, added to the purpose for which it was erected—the worship of a deity—make it the most imposing ruin I have seen. This last makes the wide differenee between it and the Coliseum, for which, had it that consecration, there would be no words. I wandered round, through it, gathered wild acanthus from crevices in its columns and clefts in its floor; gazed at the near sea at one end, passing an arm round one of its mighty symmetrical columns, not encircling it, you may be sure, as the diameter is seven and a half feet; followed the slow grazing of sheep on those once-sacred grounds; sat down on the broken and half-buried steps inside, and looked up at

Pantheon, Rome.

the intense blue of Italy's noon-day sky; went to different points around it to get every aspect of

"That noble wreck of ruinous perfection,"

and felt it impossible to sufficiently admire it. The Basilica near by is also of great magnitude, but less and not so majestic in its proportions. The third is the Temple of Ceres. It is comparatively small, but full of simple majesty. As I looked at these wonderful ruins, what most strangely moved me was an appreciation of the power and glory of man, and the recognition of what an element worship has been in the history of our race.

Another was my Sorrento day, which meant one of those ideal drives called "Cornichean," because of the road's projecting like a cornice from the headlands and precipitous hillsides. In some places, the road is cut out of the solid rock; in others, it pierces it, forming beautiful arches, but always keeping the sea in view. This kept also Ischia, Capri and Vesuvius before the charmed gaze. No other point commands such fine and complete outlines of Vesuvius—its perfect gradual upward sweep and swell from the water's edge to its cone, with the ever-rising column of smoke. Part of this drive takes its way through orange and olive groves and mulberry trees, figs, pomegranates and aloes, mingled in delicious suggestiveness. The town itself is small, and situated amid these delightful groves, rather orchards, on rocks rising abruptly from the sea, with deep ravines on the other side. It was the birthplace of Tasso; and it is said, the house in which he was born and the rock on which it stood have been swallowed up by the sea, and that the ruins are still visible beneath its clear blue waters. Nearly the entire sea-front is occupied by hotels, situated in gardens, with steps descending to the sea; and bathing establishments commanding magnificent views. We visited its shops, celebrated for their inlaid and carved wooden work and silks.

My second trial of Naples was as unsatisfactory as the first. It rained in torrents, and then I "gave up in despair." The trip from Naples back to Rome almost made me forget my grievance. It was full of historic interest and association. We passed "ancient Capua," where Spartacus led in the war of the gladiators. Just this side of it is a district so productive it yields two crops of grain and one of hay in the same season. We had a splendid view of the celebrated monastery of Monte Casino, situated on the top of a lofty hill. It is founded on the site of an ancient temple of Apollo, to which Dante alludes in his "Paradiso." Thomas Aquinas was educated there. Varro's villa was near, and it is to one of its abbots that the world is indebted for the preservation of his works. Its library is celebrated for its manuscripts, and some of them suggested to Dante his great works. In sight was Aquino, the birthplace of both Thomas Aquinas and Juvenal.

Rome. Here, in the "Eternal City." Every day is one to be chronicled. The day after I came was Palm Sunday. I went to St. Peter's to see both it and the ceremonies of the distribution of consecrated palms. I will not describe St. Peter's. Had I not already seen Westminster Abbey, St. Paul's and all the other most celebrated English cathedrals, no doubt the impression would have been overwhelming. The ceremonies were very unimposing; the music was not extraordinary; high mass was performed in one of the chapels, which dwarfed it to a very commonplace performance; and the distribution of palms was done by children, poor, forlorn-looking friars and licensed peddlers, the consecration having been previously done by one of the cardinals.

While the services were being performed in the chapel, people were walking and rambling all over the rest of the vast temple, and unless quite close to it, might have been quite unaware that anything was going on within. As no seats were provided, I went out and joined the ramblers. Presently I came upon the bronze statue of St. Peter, the toes of which are being worn away by the kisses of the devout. I found a seat and sat down to look on. Every class and grade was represented, from prince and princess to pauper and villain, the former using their dainty perfumed handkerchiefs to wipe a spot before touching their lips to it; the latter, their ragged and tainted sleeves. One young priest wiped the side of the foot and kissed it, instead of the much-imposed-upon toes.

To the end of "Holy Week," I devoted myself to seeing its various services. Each church has its special services. In that of St. Apollonari, the washing and kissing the feet of the disciples is done by a cardinal. I waited through a prolonged service of nearly four hours to witness it. There were thirteen youthful priests seated in a row on a bench raised two steps above the floor for the greater convenience of the rather too fat father. Each in succession thrust out a bare foot as he knelt, then washed, wiped, and, so far as I could see, gave an honest kiss. There was a crimson satin cushion for him to kneel on, which, however, the attending priests forgot to move along for him, so he had to use the bare floor. I was suspicious enough to think the omission was intentional. All his gorgeous vestments were removed while he was doing this, and he looked a very plain, humble creature indeed.

In another was high mass and the showing of part of the cross to which Christ was bound to be scourged. This church is opened but the once in the year, and then only to ladies. No man can enter under pain of excommunication. The other part of the cross is in Jerusalem. I urged a very agreeable elderly English lady to go to see it. For reply, she looked at me with a twinkle in her shrewd eyes, and said: "I am not going to spend my time in any such tomfoolery as that." What a homelike sound her unvarnished English had!

In yet another there was a grand ceremony of showing the heads of St. Peter and St. Paul—a ghastly spectacle at best. But the glory has departed from Catholicism in Rome.

"Holy Week" is a very tame period now-a-days. One could be here and not hear of it. Indeed, it was with great difficulty that we could get any accurate information of its program. In only one church was there a jam. The pope never shows himself; his seclusion is said to be absolute. All of the grandest spectacles and ceremonies are omitted, so "Holy Week" is rapidly ceasing to be an attraction.

We had a delightful drive on the Via Appia, that old Roman road, built three hundred and twelve years before Christ, that even to-day, is called the "queen of roads." This is the finest of the near excursions in the Campagna, the ruins of the aquaducts, mountains and villages, while the remains of ancient tombs on each side of the road are a unique and singularly fascinating feature. We took it in to visit the catacombs of St. Callistus; the tomb of CaecilliaMetella; the grotto and grove of Egeria. Stopping at the Catacombs, we were provided with wax tapers and guides and plunged down a precipitous stairway, and in a moment would have been plunged in Plutonian darkness but for these little lights that only served "to make darkness more visible." Next came threading our way through narrow, tortuous passages,

Strada dei Sepolcri (Street of Tombs), Pompeii.

single file, coming occasionally to tombs of some extent, containing the bodies of popes, saints and "other people." In several of these were paintings, the subjects of which were still quite easily made out. Some of the decorative inscriptions date as far back as the fourth century, and the frescoes to the seventh and eighth. In one chamber are two sarcophagi still containing the skeletons of the deceased, which are seen through a glass cover; one looking like a mummy, the other very much crumbled. The guide hurried us, so the visit was rather confusing, and I came out. The tomb of Caecillia Metella was a fascination to me I was scarcely prepared for, notwithstanding my remembrance of Childe Harold's famous description. To reach the Grotto of Egeria, we had to take a walk through some fields, and descend a hill into a ravine through which a little brook, the Almo, flows in an artificial channel. The Grotto is not large, but very beautiful, draped with ivy over the entire arch of the opening. On the wall facing the entrance is a mutilated statue. The fountain bursts from the wall to the right of it about four or five feet from the floor. A peasant was filling his vessels from it and he gave us a drink. It was clear, cool and of pleasant flavor. Thence a further walk along the brook and the ascent of not a very high hill, led to a grove of thick and striking ilex trees. They are of great size and evergreen. I went under every tree to be sure I did not miss that at whose roots Numa learned his lessons of wisdom.

> "Egeria, sweet creation,
> Whatsoever thy birth,
>   Thou wert a beautiful thought and softly bodied forth."

L. G. C.

Rome, April 4, 1883.

ROME.

YOU see you did right about the address, sending the letter to care of Paris banker. I have it, and it came "on time," good time, not loitering by the way or flying off at a tangent. The one point I object to is the soft rebuke to me for not having specified an address. I had given you all that I expected to. It is too much of a risk to change my address with the changes of place of such a vagrant. *Now*, stick to H. & Co., etc., till I write you to do otherwise. You will be a sharp, yes, pre-destinated fault-finder if you can hook a grumble on that. I defy you. Thanks for your appreciation of the letter! I am sure I did not mean anything so extraordinary. You say so many pleasant things, I cannot ignore them, as is my wont. I hope you are like Lady Geraldine, who

> "Said such good things natural,
> As if she always thought them."

Anyhow, it is wonderfully exhilarating to

feel I have put out the Bermuda burner. Her scintillations were vastly oppressive.

I have recently been reveling in Guercino's fresco of Aurora, widely different from Guido's famous one, but I think I like it quite as much. Aurora herself is the central figure, a lovely, radiant creature embodying all the glimmer, glow and glamor of the dawn, seated in her car drawn by two splendid steeds. mottled with the dusk they were scattering and the light they were heralding. She was dropping flowers as she sped onward; a lovely cherub hovered in the air before stretching chaplets of exquisite flowers toward her; another, nestling in the cloudy folds of her drapery behind, looked over the edge of the car right into my eyes with his that seemed just as living. Do not tell on me; but I make rosebuds of my lips at him every time we catch each other's eyes, and he seems to enjoy the pantomine. Just in front of the horses' heads, the earliest hours, bewitching young maidens, are putting out the stars, each with extended forefinger and thumb, flashing lightly up to the pretty sparks. It looks the most fascinating "task to do." You cannot help feeling a quiver in your own fingers to try it. Away ahead of all a bat is flying from the coming

ROME. 253

light. You think in a flash of that beautiful song:

> "Come into the garden, Maud,
> The black bat, Night, is fled."

And now the quiver in my finger is gone:

I have put out that transcendant Star that made a "vexed Bermoothes" of *me!*

And I hope Guercina's manes will take no offense at this association of ideas!

Ah! this imperial Rome—this unapproachable queen of the earth—every day I am more and more overcome by "the toils of her beauty" and enchantments. The magic of yesterday is lost in that of to-day; and for that of to-morrow I shall be dumb, having no words to express it. I wonder how anyone can ever get free from her wonderful fetters forged of everything that adds charm to life. From the deep blue of its sky, the crystalline dazzle of its atmosphere, the unutterable fusion "of all the hues of all the earth," and the varied outline of hill and vale and mount and wide-spread campagna—all this, just the mere outside, the physical Rome, to her treasures of myths, history, etc., everything you know, why attempt to enumerate? She is in everything—"Mistress of the World." I, for one, am her willingest, lealest, lovingest subject or slave, as you will. It seems to me at times as if of all I have ever known there is nothing very worthy that has not some associations with her. Living within her walls brings out all that was written long ago on the memory, but grown from the lapse of time and the swift succession of experiences into an "invisible writing," as it were. Yes, brings it out just as heat will bring that out. At every turn there is a great name, or some great monument of the mighty dead, and as you pause to look you ponder and remember what made the name great, who built the great monument, who indeed were the mighty dead! Sometimes you know so much it is a kind of intoxicating joy. Oh! yes; many times—most times of course, you know so little.

Do not think of being afraid or ashamed of admitting that. And then such a hunger and thirst as takes possession of you for knowledge, more knowledge, and yet more and more. The hunger and thirst of one perishing in the desert can but faintly shadow this forth. You think of that wonder-story of Eve, and the condemnation of her that has been a birth-right and grown with your orthodox growth, insensibly softens into sympathy. Presently you will find yourself admitting you too might have—yes, would have eaten that apple! For it meant—knowledge, more knowledge! I— I— am shocking you. Well, come thou also, and see if it be possible not to rave—

. . . .

Are you in the mood for a tramp? Come, let's be off. There is an old church—*S. Onofrio*, on the slope of the Janiculus we ought to see. It is off to the west, no great distance from St. Peter's. The *Salita* (or ascent) is steep. It is a warm, relaxing day—do not go too fast; you will get into a perspiration if you do, and then you will have to take care of a breeze or a draught, and maybe catch cold, after all. Best not hurry. What is there up there, anyhow? *Why*—ever so many things you would not miss for—anything. The quaintest old structure dating from 1439—ahead of America! and built in honor of Honophrius, whose story is disgusting to me; but let that go. Here is what I like better. Tasso lived there—I do not know how long—and died there. The whole place is far more full of, and fragrant with, his memory than that of the saint. The chapel in which he is buried has an immense affair in the way of a monument. It is not considered a work of "high art," so we shall not linger.

Here in a chapel beside his is the tomb of Mezzofanti, the linguist; a simple slab in the floor, with the name and dates. I like it. Somehow I am in such a fever to go on. I do not care much for the pictures, though some have great names. Here—through this corridor. It leads to the "cell" which Tasso occupied and in which he died. The custodian opens the door. I step in first, and involuntarily step back. Facing me is a full-length fresco portrait of the poet on the wall, so life-like, for the moment the illusion is complete. In the center of the room is his bust. It was taken from the cast of his face in death; it is in a glass case. On the wall behind is another glass case, in which is an autograph letter, much tattered and torn and yellow with age. There are also his gloves, belt, etc. Ranged against the wall and protected by a railing are some large, square, leather-covered chairs, in frames of oak or walnut, with gold-gilt ornamentation. On another side, also in a large glass cabinet, is the coffin in which he was first interred. The "cell" itself is a good-sized room, with three windows, two commanding fine, extensive views. There is a garden attached, with a riven oak, the remains of that under which Tasso used to sit. We must go and sit there too. The walk lies between large beds of growing vegetables. You see ahead your goal—a sharp little rise, from the side of which, half-way up, leans out remains of the tree. On one side is an old wall, rather a fragment; on the other, some steep, high steps, up which you know you will have to toil "for the view." Almost in a breath you are doing it, and—ugh! at every step a swarm of glancing lizards! I cry: "Look out for the lizards!" A lady ahead of me, already at the top, seated on a part of the wall, says coolly, if encouragingly: "You know they are harmless. Why are you afraid?" I protest: "I am not afraid; but a lady carried one home with her yesterday in the folds of her skirts, and it was there ever so long, I know. I don't wish the experience of a lizard for a vade mecum." So I gather my skirts close and above my boot-tops, and do not miss the view indeed; but neither do I those legions in their brilliant uniform of green spotted with gold. And the view! St. Peter's on the left, still farther west; the city to the east, with its innumerable domes and spires; and far beyond, the beautiful mountains, some of their tops lost in the blue mist; and overhead, the broad arms of the oak, with their budding sprays. The warm air makes you feel a curious languor. You too sit down, feeling as if you were swooning into that noontide. Only a moment, though—those lizards!

It is time to go. You make the circuit of the gnarled roots; try to break off a bit of the riven edges, to find them as hard as adamant; look up and sigh to find the leaves quite beyond reach; then turn away for good and all. After a step or so, you find you are still clutching at your skirts! And as you reach the walk again, the other lady looks back and says meekly and deprecatingly, "I feel as if I had a thousand lizards on me." One can forgive the answering peal of laughter; it is meriment only, not triumph. Then both gave wings to their feet! Can *you* keep up? I lay a wager you think you can!

Then another *prowl*. Do you not want to see that statue of Pompey, "at whose base Great Caesar fell?" I have thought of it and of "Great Caesar" many times. Indeed, it is one of the first thoughts when one sees the forum. The statue is in the Palazzo Spada; is in an immense ante-room. It needs to be, so

Quirinal, Rome.

colossal is the statue. The workmanship is not considered very fine, but a strong interest must always attach to it on account of the association. The Palazzo is well situated, but it is near the Jew quarter called the Ghetto, and which is one of the characteristic sights. The street is narrow and tortuous, winding between houses six and seven stories high. The dwellers live literally out-doors, for even if inside the house, it is all wide open. The women are sitting, plying their various avocations, all seeming to be made up in some way of old, filthy clothes. The men are roving about just as busily. The children are at play so thick, there is some discretion required to enable one to thread his way without stepping on them. All are unkempt, unwashed, unattractive. Both smells and looks are revolting. Curiosity is soon satisfied. We hurry. Just ahead of us is the house of Rienzi, and near by a pretty little ruined temple called that of Vesta; these are on the bank of the Tiber, and just at the foot, as it were, of the Palatine. Further on is the Protestant cemetery, where are buried Keats and the *heart* of Shelley. I have been to both. Fresh flowers were lying on the slab over the latter, while the grave of Keats was a mass of sweet violets. There is a neat hedge around it, and everything betokens kindly and constant care. Poor fellow! His name is *not* written in water. Oh! but I must break off. There is no end to all I wish I could tell you. I sympathize with you in the loss of that lovely woman, Mrs. D——. Such a frail, tender life; the wonder is it has lasted so long. I had heard something of what you mention. Believe

> "It is better to have loved and lost
> Than never to have loved at all."

Yes, the added verse is an immortality. May I indeed be there to hear, and all our "beautiful beloved" who have gone before. You did not mention our dear one, Miss B——. Do you know anything about her? I have had no letter since I wrote to you, but so many of my letters do not reach me, I attach no blame to her, only I wish so much to hear. And will you make the race for governor? If so, I will put up special prayers for your election. Then if you are elected, you will invite us two to visit you in that castle made without hands. Won't you, please. Thanking you for all your kindly expressions and injunctions.

L. G. C.

Rome, April 24, 1883.

ROME.

IN Rome still, but this is my last week. Were I to write many books, I could not get in the half of these wonder days in this queen city of the world. Yes, crowned so long ago, she still wears her royal diadem, and will wear it even as the old lines have it:

"While Rome stands, the world stands!"

I have made the rounds of the churches, that of the galleries and museums, that of the villas and palaces, and finally that of the—shops. Take notice, that of the studios, is omitted; not because it was not made, but because it was confined to four. Such a four, though! One can hardly realize any were left out. Be sure they will come in for ample mention. Will it seem sacrilegious to admit several hours of one afternoon were devoted to the Lateran, and the rest to watching the queen and "lesser mortals" coming home from the races? Life is a very mixed sort of affair here—"Motley's the wear," in-

indeed, and there's nothing to be done but "Being in Rome to do as Romans do." The only saving clause is I did not hurry through the church because of the carnival ahead.

I began with the Piazza di San Giovanni and its great obelisk—"the largest in existence," erected some fifteen hundred years ago by an Egyptian king in front of the Temple of the Sun, at Thebes. I felt that it had strayed "far away from its native heath." This is one of eleven obelisks brought from far eastern climes to grace this imperial city. The conqueror has a right to his spoils, I suppose, or this might be called vandalism. In the Baptistery, I saw the font of green basalt in which tradition says Constantine was baptized; and in its several chapels, Mosaic frescoes dating as far back as the Fifth century. They were more curious than beautiful, the figures representing Christ, apostles and saints, being decidedly of a caricature order. But one—flowers and birds on a gold ground, and another—golden arabesques on a blue ground—were more successful, indeed beyond criticism. I lingered long at the foot of Santa Scala, "that flight of twenty-eight marble steps from the palace of Pilate at Jerusalem, which Christ is said to have ascended once," and which are now set aside for the devout to ascend on their knees only. Many were doing it as I watched—men, women and children; old and young; rich and poor. To the looker-on it would seem rather an acrobatic feat, than an act of devotion.

At five o'clock, we took our station on the wayside, one of a "jam" of carriages to wait for the coming of the royal cortege! In the intervals of waiting, I amused myself pointing out the coroneted equipages; they clustered around, their occupants apparently quite as eager as we to see the spectacle. Presently the chatter was hushed; eye-glasses of all kinds were adjusted; everybody's gaze was on the Porta San Giovanni; a flash of scarlet shot through its arch; the jockey who always precedes the queen's carriage, itself with its four steeds, most richly caparisoned—the coachman and two footmen in the brilliant scarlet uniform of the queen; and inside, the beautiful, gracious, happy-looking Marguerite, a queen indeed, if looks and bearing count! She bowed so queenly, and smiled so womanly, right and left, I no longer wonder that her subjects worship her. A number of gorgeous equipages followed; the pageant swept on, and the chill dusk hurried us home.

Another church was the qaint old building of St. Onofrio, on the Janiculus. It was reared to commemorate the piety of that saint, shown by a life of sixty years' hermitage in the desert, reducing himself to the level of the brute creation. I confess my pilgrimage to his shrine was not from sympathy with any such idea of piety. Nor has it much in the way of art. Three frescoes by Domenichino, and one fresco, faded and injured by retouching, by Leonardo da Vinci, are all worth speaking of. But Tasso is buried there, and the cell he occupied is shown, full of souvenirs of him. It is a large room, with three windows, and commands some fine views. The souvenirs are a fresco portrait of him, life-size and most startlingly life-like; a bust in wax, autograph letters, chairs, etc. There is a garden attached, in which is an oak under which he used to sit. The view from that "coigne de vantage" is lovely. I seated myself where he might have sat to enjoy it. But—you have read about the pretty, glancing, green and gold lizards of Italy! Well, it seemed to me there was one at least to every blade of grass, to every twig, where anything could glide or dangle. A lady had carried one home with her the day before in the folds of her dress. I was not very ambitious to follow her example, so, perhaps very ingloriously, I decamped without delay.

There is a set of churches, three in number, called "The Three Churches of the Aventine," from their being situated on that hill. Each has something of special interest, but I shall tell of only one, that of St. Sabrina. It contains Sassoferrato's masterpiece, the "Madonna of the Rosary," a really beautiful and interesting picture of this inexhaustible subject. The Madonna is giving a rosary to St. Dominicus, and the Christ-child another to St. Catherine; the latter with a childlike delight and benevolence in the giving, most admirably rendered. On the pillar in the nave is a good-sized black bowlder, with the legend attached that it was hurled by the devil at St. Dominicus when at prayer; such was his fury at this pious act. The flagstone on which the saint was kneeling was also shown. It has been removed from the floor and built into the wall. There is an orange tree in the garden, still vigorous and beautiful, planted by St. Dominicus. The good brothers make crosses and rosaries of its wood and sell them, thus "making an honest penny." We bought some and took them to the pope to be consecrated!

This prowling about old churches, hunting up celebrated pictures, relics, legends, etc., comes to be a great fascination. As they are counted by hundreds, one can always have a place to go. The trouble is to make a selection. And—it is just as perplexing which to tell you about. There is one more, though, I do not like to leave out. It is small and not at all striking; stands beside the great Doria palace on the Corso, and right in the way, but comparatively few enter it. The name is St. Maria in Via Lata, and it is the church in which St. Paul and St. Luke taught.

There are really two churches, one entered from the street and the other beneath it, reached by descending a flight of steps. The latter is the one where the apostles preached, and very small and humble and dark; the custodian carried lighted tapers to insure our seeing. There were some faded frescoes on the walls, a well, the water of which burst forth miraculously for the baptism of converts under their preaching; and there is a fragment of the ancient Servian wall in one end that is very curious, with its huge blocks of stone arranged both upright and horizontally. In the upper church is preserved that remarkable picture of the head of Christ "begun by St. Luke and finished by an angel." It is kept closely shut up in a cabinet over the alter, but a silver lira won an inspection. Faded, dingy, crude, all that can be said is that neither of the accredited artists could have worked from especial training or inspiration! From churches to studios—a natural transition. What galleries the former have been, and are, for the latter.

Strolling through the Via Margutta—"the artist's quarter"—a large building arrested attention. On inquiring, we found, among many other studios in it, those of our Rodgers and Ives. Applying quite unceremoniously for admittance to the first, was accorded at once, and the son of Mr. Rodgers advanced and received us most courteously, and conducted us through several rooms, full of the completed works of his father, and a number of work-rooms full of busy workmen. Among the many admirable finished works, four particularly interested us: "The Lost Pleiad," "Ruth," "Somnambulist" and "The Blind Girl of Pompeii." Never was the groping movement peculiar to the blind so touchingly rendered as in that slight, girlish figure. She is pressing forward against a strong wind, which is shown by the way her hair and skirts are blown backward, grasping her staff, and feeling her way equally, as it were, with it, and the sightless orbs directed so intently before her. What a curious mastery of the "cold, insensate marble" that can make the heart ache so!

We were equally unceremonious and fortunate in our reception at the studio of Mr. Ives. He was just going out, but turned at once, and accompanied us with the utmost kindness and graciousness through his rooms. There, too, were many well-filled, and others where the workmen's chisels were busy. It was interesting to pause and watch the tiny chips and threads of marble dust as made under their skillful touches, and mark the delicate finish given thereby to lip and brow, the more tender curve to the dainty shoulder, the more graceful sweep to the trailing drapery. I gazed longest on a "young Bacchus," a drooping "Ariadne," that half elf, half human "Undine," and that nymph of wood, water and wisdom, "Egeria." The last, especially, drew me to it again and again. It is a sitting statue inclining somewhat forward, gazing earnestly at the right foot extending before it, and from the toes of which streams of water are gushing. The left foot is drawn back and is resting on the tip of the toes. There is little drapery, but the little is exquisitely wrought. The features are of ethereal beauty; the hair is arranged in a simple Grecian knot. She is sitting on a stump entwined with ivy; around its roots the wild acanthus spreads its beautiful leaves. The lovely creature! I think it will haunt me forever.

The third studio was that of an Italian artist. Besides his pictures, the rooms were adorned with tapestries, rugs and bric-a-brac. There were some most ingenious exhibitions of taste. In one room the light fell on crayons on glass, most attractive pictures. Passing to another room behind this, the light shone through these, converting them into exquisite transparencies. It was a desire to light what would have been otherwise a dark room, without marring the walls of the others by introducing windows. There were some portraits on his walls, wonderful as paintings, and carrying conviction of their faithfulness as likenesses. One was a queenly woman, with that splendid texture of flesh so often described by the words, "you can almost see the bones through it," because of its transparency, features " clean cut as a cameo," a warm fine glow on the cheek; elsewhere that pinkish pearl hue of youth and health; and heavy masses and braids of the richest golden hair, with the very glint of the burnished metal on it. I felt like plucking out a strand or two that they might never be turned to silver, and thinking of Aurora Leigh, kept asking myself "how many ingots went to make that dazzling sheen?" So realistic was this "vision of beauty," one could easily believe it would turn and answer, did you speak to it.

It was, however, the last studio of the four where I went oftenest and lingered longest, and always with increasing pleasure—that of Dwight Benton, formerly of Cincinnati, and who favors the "Commercial" now and then with a delightful letter. Doubtless you have read them. His studio consists of two spacious rooms, most admirably lighted and tastefully fitted up. It is a gallery in itself, with its walls covered with "studies," and its many easels filled with wonder-works of his never idle brush! Of late years he paints landscapes exclusively, and it may be added "con amore." Such enthusiasm is bound to tell—so there are scenes from Capri that do not seem to belong to canvass at all—that strip of beach is there to stroll on; those cliffs you will climb sooner or later; the chickens aroost in the little boat drawn up in the shadow of a corner of that quaint old house, will have to fly for it by and by, when you will want it for a sail; in a few moments you are going up the steps to follow that tall, stately-looking peasant woman just disappearing in that old house, for you are eager to explore it. You look further! On another easel is a stretch of the Campagna, seen beyond and through some near ruins. There are patches of sunlight on the grass, not paint, but the warm, intangible sunbeams that drop from the sky to the earth—that wonderful Campagna! It rolls away in shifting arabesques and mosaics of all the hues

> "That in the colors of the rainbow live
> And play in the plighted clouds,"

till afar off it strikes that line of mountains, with their top lost in great masses of tossing, seething storm-clouds, or veiled in depth after depth of bluest mist. It seems as if he had wrenched the reality itself from the out-door world, and flung it on the canvass. The gaze wanders from one easel to another with long pauses at each. How I wish I could do them the faintest justice with any words of mine. I can give the subjects and the features, but those miracles of atmospheric effects wrought apparently with as little effort by this artist's brush as if by enchantment—it is those that are unutterable, indescribable, and must be seen by one's own eyes. I consider myself most fortunate in having secured two of his smaller canvasses "to be a possession forever." The larger is a Capri scene of coast and cliff; the white-crested waves are rolling in gently, and breaking upon the former; the ruins of the palace of Tiberius crown the latter. It is a picture of striking individuality and specially characteristic of this foreign world. The other is a subject of pathetic interest, which he calls "Shelley's grave." It represents the coast near Spezzia, where the body of the poet was washed ashore, found and interred for a time. A simple cross marks the grave. A somber sky, the low coast, a little strip of beach, the grass and weeds and sedgy growth peculiar to such a spot, with a rude cross, that is all. But what a story it tells! So anxious am I that others may have an opportunity to see and appreciate this home artist, I shall make a special point with my old friends of the book-store of The Robert Clarke Company, Cincinnati, of having these placed in their windows as soon as they reach the United States. One so gifted in his profession, and of such high worth in every phase of character as Mr. Benton, should have most ample recognition from his fellow-countrymen.

L. G. C.

Rome, May 2, 1883.

MAIORI.

DO not trouble to tell me: I know I have been delinquent. But then that is not one of my "too many and too-tedious-to-make-mention of feelings." So the one time can be blinked at. Especially if you remember the scripture injunction. If you are like me you never do unless you want to.

Of course your letter came and I had my habitual "good intentions," but well, to be honest, I am sure I do not know what became of them. I only realize that the days "shod with silver speech," and muzzled with golden speechlessness, have slipped away and given no warning, till I should be afraid to try to count them. Let them go, and be magnanimous enough to bear no malice. That comes so easy to me I can recommend it without any tinges of that inward monitor yclept conscience. It would be the 13th labor of Hercules to attempt to fill up this interval. My brain reels at the mere mention. But I will just give you a mosaic of random tiles. You will like it just as well.

In any case you would feel called on to groan critically and perhaps cry aloud: "The old flippancy! What a butterfly she is." You know I do not mind.

One of the party, the "lord of creation," you may be sure, had the fever at Rome, to his supreme disgust, not the Roman, but typhoid. He was sick two months. This, of course, was a cloud. But he is a darling, and just to get him well again was our supreme anxiety. As soon as he was well enough to travel without risk, he was ordered here to escape Roman lassitude and be "built up." Last Monday we started, "coming by easy stages." Naples was our first resting-place. We remained till Saturday. By that date the invalid through much eating and drinking shed even the role of a convalescent, and "Richard is himself again," was asserted in every look and act. But we have come on here all the same. I wish you could spend just one day if no more with us. Such a dream-place as it is! Words can never picture it to you, but the cousins in chorus, declared I must write and tell *you* all about it. As if I could! Why *you?* They did not say. I did not ask. I *suppose* because they are ready to hear another of your letters read. You see they have not such a funny, audacious correspondent as you on their list.

But to this "castle in Spain," this "Palace Beautiful," this "stately pleasure dome," this "Dream Perch," this "Hotel Torre di Mezzacapo," on the "blue Meditterranean's" loveliest inlet, the Gulf of Salerno. Oh, dear. How to put it into words! It is an ancient castle, built on and out of, and into, a lofty cliff, hanging right over the water. I could cast my lines into its clear depths and *angle* to no end of capture, if they were long enough. They would have to measure 90 meters (300 feet) though to touch water. Who would help me land my whales? A Cornichean road, the ideal highway of creation, winds past its base to Amalfi. I hope you know Longfellow's poem of that name. Sheer down the solid rock drops to the wavelets' foam-tipped caress. I can *hear* them when I bend over the parapet of my terrace so high above them in the air. From that highway, superb-macadamized, the ascent to our doorway is a tortuous, devious, steep climb. A little donkey-cart does it. Two at a time inside, outside the driver alongside the poor beast and with a desperate clutch of its loose hide to help it to keep its feet, and like poor Joe, "keep moving on." As I caught sight of that grip, a flash of memory gave back a description read long ago, of an exceedingly high-bred aristocratic, "black and tan terrier—its skin was at least two and one-half sizes too large for it." Poor little donkey! I can fancy him braying his loudest that dying refrain of the woman,

"Glory! hallelujah! I am going where
There's no more hard work to do."

After he landed the four of us "safe and sound," he dragged up with equal faithfulness our four "Saratogas." When I saw that, I cowered into a corner and hid my eyes. How I hated that trunk of mine! I think that particular donkey ought to be canonized and made a "constellation" in one of the unoccupied places of honor in the sky. Up here we see "an inclosed world of beauty." The vague distance of the sea, where the eye gets lost directly; the long, low promontory or cape, where Paestum lies stranded in blue mist; mountains that lift themselves up so high they win crowns of snow for their temerity; great, soaring, jagged, curiously rent cliffs, many with their sheltered sides fashioned into terraces set in fruitful lemon and orange groves; the indented coast, with many a pretty bay and baylet and little stretches of exquisite beaches; and countless villages in the tenderest tones of white, gray, drab, etc. It is a wonderful scene, and so soporific I could fall asleep this very instant. It is Sunday all the time. The town of Maiori lies far below us on the northeast, with a population of six thousand, an exquisite bit of harbor and lovely beach. I see pretty little craft, of many styles and sizes, run up on the last. Now and then, out on the water, a microscopic sail attached to a little black speck, or a lazily propelled row-boat, breaks up "the death in life" of the scene. They tell me as a fact that can be verified, of other *breaks* of the following ilk, *if* one chooses to hang by the hour over the parapet of the different terraces or esplanades: a rattle-trap of a wagon, with a team of three animals abreast, mixed horses and donkeys, or oxen and cows, but each one close kin to my poor "Raffaello" (that is our donkey's name); a tourist carriage or donkey cart; or a procession of "beasts of burden," with immense baskets, heaping full, or casks of wine and water, or some miscellaneous burden, borne on top of their heads, and heavy enough to bend them half-double at least—in the shape of *women*. Oftentimes men walk beside, but never seem to share those burdens.

Maiori lies at the mouth of a gorge, the Val Tramonti. This runs (I don't know how far) back through a volcanic district. There is an ascending drive that is singularly unique and interesting. On both sides, a jumble of rent mountains; upheavals of beautiful knolls, that would themselves be mountains elsewhere, in the center of vast basins and deep valleys. Capping many of the highest peaks are lone, picturesque, gray old churches, with tall, square towers. The sides of the mountains are laid out in terraces, covered with lemon groves or orchards. Continuous chains of quaint old towns nestle in the depths or perch at different altitudes, so varied in their styles of architecture, combination of colors, and situations framed in such a novel ensemble, one is kept in a glow all the way. All this region abounds with such drives.

Verily, if this modicum of a world is so full of wonders, it is crushing to try to grasp the stupendous creation of which it is so small a fraction.

We shall stay here, exploring, perhaps a fortnight; and then to "fresh fields."

There is talk of Sicily and Africa, if it continues cool enough.

And to make last week one to "set apart," my "good brother," Mr. W——, reached me with one of his letters. There are a sacred few who keep us at our best. The angel—not the demon—in us answers to their summons. Just to be with them seems to banish whatsoever is unworthy. Heaven—the All-good—seems not far away, hedged off from entrance by this and that device of man; but all about us, with its paths ready and free to our treading, and its true life not withdrawing and making conditions of acceptance, but enfolding and making us feel it is our own inheritance and we can enter into it.

I hope the little book is growing or quite grown. It interests me to hear of it. Do not give it up, whatever you do.

I noted the recovery of your peculiar and pretty penmanship the moment I saw your letter. Blessed be the potato, henceforth and forever!

L. G. C.

Maiori, April 5, 1886.

Naples, General View.

NAPLES.

I THINK I told you Sicily was being talked of for our next objective point. Well, we had a beautiful drive to Salerno; from there by rail to Paestum, where I enjoyed the grand old temples for the second time, the others for the first time.

We lunched in the temple of Neptune, and I gathered again the acanthas and wild flowers. The trip was charming, through a continuous garden with orchards and farm lands.

At the temple, an incident occurred I do not like to recall. I was looking at some curios surrounded by a throng of boys of all ages. While deciding about purchasing a very peculiar terra cotta head, they pressed closer and closer to me. Presently I wanted my glasses; they were gone. I could not linger. Before we reached the station, they were brought to me; had evidently been taken from my pocket for that very purpose, with the certainty of getting a reward. This was the only instance of the kind that happened to me in all my wanderings.

Back to Salerno, and from there to Pompeii. The whole route was a revel of spring beauty. Deep valleys, mountains, wide-spreading plains—"how beautiful and wonderful all this little earth!" We spent the time till train hour for Naples in the exhumed city. Nothing more marvelous than its frescoes so fresh and well-preserved.

Naples and shopping next day. Some friends who had just returned from Sicily and Tunis came to tell us about it. One brought many Tunis purchases to show us. Another gave a description of a Tunis wedding, which, by a happy chance, they witnessed. The bride did not see her husband for eight days! The display of presents was most gorgeous.

At 4 p. m., we went to the steamer for Sicily. A storm was brewing as we boarded it, and by the late dinner hour it was upon us in all its fury. One by one the passengers left the table till I alone remained. The effect on me was not ordinary sea-sickness, but a kind of torpidity; once in my birth I could not lift my head, though I was not unconscious. The storm lasted all night, but the morning broke brilliantly clear and invigorating.

Palermo at noon; we had to stay aboard

Peasant Cart, Palermo.

till 3 p. m., to be put through a process of disinfecting. All sorts of officers came to examine. Barges ran alongside with great tubs of disinfectant water to put soiled clothes through. Then the dogano, and such a racket of talk and cries! Hotel des Palmes from the steamer. It was pleasantly situated and very comfortable, and has a lovely garden. Before going to bed, Tunis was given up. The cousins could not risk the sea-sickness.

We spent several days in Palermo and its environs. I think it might be called the City of Mosaics. Its cathedrals, chapels, palaces, walls, everywhere were a mass of this ornamentation. We went from one to another till my brain was in a buzz. The gorgeousness and beauty and exquisite execution of the extraordinary subjects were beyond description. Only seeing can grasp such wonders. There was an *English garden* full of flowers and familiar and unfamiliar trees and shrubbery. Indeed, Palermo can boast many gardens. In our drives on the Marina, a very brilliant feature was the carts peculiar to the country. The body of the cart, the two wheels, the shafts and the trappings of the donkey were covered with pictures and designs in the gaudiest colors—blues, reds, greens, orange, etc. The peasants in them were arrayed in garb to match, with faces alight with the most good-humored smiles.

The palaces we were most interested in were those of La Zisa and La Cuba, of Saracenic origin. The feature of the former was its fountain bursting from the wall in the vestibule facing the entrance door, and descending over a succession of steps to the floor, where it took the form of a simple rectangular cross. Above the fountain was a painted arch, below which were three pictures in Mosaics. This was very curious. La Cuba had nothing but a discolored honey-combed vaulting in a small court. A pavilion formerly belonging to it had been removed to the center of a garden on the opposite side of the street. We tramped to it. It had a dome in the roof and an arched doorway, and was built of massive stones, but otherwise was not especially interesting.

To Monreale was a drive of several miles, to see its Cathedral and Abbey and fine views. Its Mosaics are celebrated, but I did not dream of anything like the wonderful Cloisters of the Abbey. The Mosaics on the walls of the Cathedral cover an area of 70,000 square feet,

Interior of Museum (Metopes), Palermo.

representing scenes from both the Old and New Testaments. I could only look and exclaim.

The Cloisters are all that remain of the original Abbey; they are quadrangular and the pointed arches supported by 216 columns are covered with mosaics, all of their capitals and many of the shafts being different. I could not even faintly grasp the amount of labor required for the execution of such elaborate work. We had haze, showers and rain every day, but lost no time from our sight-seeing. One day we went in the rain to the Museum, where are the famous Metopes, "the most ancient of Greek sculptures except the lions of Mycene." These are from the temple of Selinus, where we were to have gone, but a party of English, who had just returned, gave such a disenchanting account of the hardships of the trip, we gave it up. These Metopes are on a sublime scale representing the contests of gods and goddesses and heroes, and are indescribable. One is that of Perseus slaying Medusa.

Not tiring of beautiful Palermo, but of the rain, we left one afternoon for Girgenti, "the most beautiful city of mortals," according to Pindar. The railway must have been the work of friendly genii, taste, labor and abundance of the "coin of the county," for it ran for miles between tripple hedges of roses, geraniums and cacti, planted in the order I have named them one above the other.

In Holland the hedges are of poppies, and "Out West" in our own country, of sunflowers, both such a blaze of color, the one red, the other orange, as to almost scorch the eye.

The number of ruins of temples on a grand scale in and around Girgenti keeps the sightseers "on the wing;" and at bed-time, the second in the little day-book reads: What a full and interesting day! I wish I had time to tell of these in detail. But Syracuse and the Fountain of Arethusa! Thither the route was of the most varied. Hills and wide-spreading vales like our prairies; cities crowning mountains; sulphur-works and great blocks of it piled at the stations ready for shipment; orchards, exquisite gardens and vineyards, but no forests, only a few trees here and there, principally eucalyptus that have been recently set out. Wild flowers by the acre in countless varieties, one being a species of clover, the head three, four and five inches long, and blood-red in color. We stopped at Catania for lunch at the station, ordered it, and when it was served with one glance let it "severely alone." Whereupon the waiter fell into a deep dejection. We reached Syracuse at 9:30 p. m.

The night drive through the streets to the hotel was beautiful, and we slept the sleep of those who knew the good things of this world were awaiting us next morning. What a day we made of it! We rambled through the Roman Ampitheater; sat where the nobles had in the Greek Theater; visited the quarries— quarries are one of the most famous characteristics of Syracuse—Euryalis, the fountain of Arethusa, indeed, leaving nothing unseen. In the quarry of Paradise is the famous Ear of Dionysius. You may be sure we tried its extraordinary echoes. In another, that of Latonia de Cappuccini, quarry of the Capuchins, we lunched. The manager of our hotel was our cicerone, a refined and gentlemanly person, but we could not induce him to join us, so strong was his feeling of the difference in our positions. He served us with gloved hands, and when we had finished withdrew from sight to take his lunch. We walked around the ruined fort atop of it, and descended into the depths of its subterranean fortifications. From the top, Mt. Etna was a sublime spectacle—its vast mass of snow-covered volcano seemed lifted bodily into the loftiest heights of air while its base was enveloped in an impenetrable white mist. Anything more ideally ethereal could not be imagined.

The Fountain of Arethusa is inclosed in a circular basin, and can be gazed upon from above standing on a platform with a railing. I looked and longed to get nearer. The custodian was at hand with key ready to unlock a gate. I entered and found the familiar quotation a truth, "Facilis est discensus." The water was edged with a thick growth of the papyrus, its long, slender stalks topped with a kind of palm-like tuft. There was a most enchanting walk from our hotel to the fountain, and an irresistible fascination found me repeating my visit to it. It took in one of the finest views of the harbor and Mt. Etna. I often stopped as I wandered to wonder if perchance I trod in the footsteps of Archimides, if my glance rested on the same points in both land and water view, and wished—how I wished!—my brain might burn with his momentous thoughts and calculations.

Exquisite views await and arrest the traveler everywhere in Sicily. There are some barren stretches, but these seem to be forgotten

Archimedes.

as soon as lost sight of. As our train swept on, these were unrolled before us. Afar off, nestling on the side of a mountain, we caught a glimpse of Meliti, where the Hybla honey of the poets was made. Once more at Catania— it seemed almost a miracle—we were ushered into a Pullman palace car! We could hardly credit "the evidence of our senses." No cars are comparable for comfort, convenience and elegance with those of our own native land. It was really amusing to see how soon we adjusted ourselves to the accustomed luxuries. We ascertained on inquiry that this was a special train placed at the expense of the Pullman Company as an experiment. It was hoped and thought it would be a success.

Directly there was a chorus of exclamation, The seven rocks of the Cyclops! The rocks the blind Polyphemus hurled so impatiently after "the crafty Ulysses." They rise at no great distance from the shore, and from the size of some of them the strength of the giant must have been indeed taxed.

Speeding over the plain of Catania took me back to school days and my mythology. For to a part of it belongs the touching story of Proserpine and its harrowing pictures of Pluto carrying her off, her arms outstretched for rescue, and her lovely face furrowed with such terror, horror and agony as fixed itself indelibly upon memory. "The Vale of Enna," with its flowers bedewed with the tears of the tortured mother and lighted by the burning torch in her hand, as she sought hither and thither for her lost child—how strange to think I was recalling all the story right there upon the ground.

We made but a short tarry at Messina, and then came our reluctant *addio* to beautiful, historic Sicily. Trinacria of old, so called because of its triangular shape. Not anywhere was flaunted that hideous coat of arms—the head of Medusa, the Gorgon with locks of wreathing serpents and the three legs springing from it as a center, representing a triangle, and the haunting countenance of horror that turned one into stone but to look at it. Yet, I put the picture of it into my album of Sicilian photographs!

How the heart aches over the good-byes that we know mean forever.

Good-bye, O lovely Sicily.

L. G. C.

Naples, May 1, 1886.

Head of Medusa, Coat of Arms of Sicily, Palermo.

LAUTERBRUNNEN.

YOURS of 15th received yesterday. May 17th was the date of receipt of your last previous favor. May 23d I mailed a reply from Florence. Yet you say you have had no letter for three months. What does this mean? I am "wrought up," I can tell you; because *that* letter was the quintessence of myself. No use to go into details about it. *You,* who so adequately wreak me upon expression, "witty, wise, brilliant, great head and good heart"— dear me! were I the most egotistical instead of meek and lowly minded of women—impossible to compete with you in *doing justice* to myself —you would resent such "poaching in your preserves." So I leave you to gnash teeth over the loss you can so fully comprehend. I shall never get over it myself, never. I think I must mention two items. There was a poem by myself and another by my cousin, Mrs. O——. I sent the latter to prove that I do not "monopolize the family genius." You will remember you put that query. Please make a note of my magnanimity in not withholding an evidence of its being possessed in even a higher degree by another member. Do you think many—not women, but—fellow-beings would be equal to that? Oh! I groan to think of that lost scintilation! And shall every time I think of it. How you would have enjoyed it! And more—how you would have flashed back again! Being the cause of wit in others is almost better than being witty myself. No; come to think of it, I have to "own up" to preferring to being the possessor at first hand, and even in the overtopping degree. There's the milk and meekness of human coveteousness, of which I am "a bright and shining light." Not much of the goddess in such a confession. But—"I can't tell a lie," you know, any more than *you* or the rest of my brethren and sisters. Oh! oh!—oh—h—h! that letter!

I am so glad you had "a good time" with Miss B——. How near she is to my heart you must know by this time.

I have had a letter since you saw her. She wrote after her return home in a glow of fine spirits. What a "triumphal progress" she and Mrs. K—— had! Everybody, everywhere, seeming to have vied in the kindliest courtesies, hospitalities and affectionate attentions. It did me as much good to hear of it as if I had myself been a recipient. Mrs. K—— deserved the hospitalities in a special degree, her pleasant home in Covington having always been a real Kentucky "open house." As for Miss B——, her extraordinary powers of entertaining—that big head of hers so stuffed full of everything that adds to the feast and festival and highest enjoyment—she honors her welcomes. Some day I count on seeing the work you are giving so much time to. The "aim" must be indeed "a difficult thing to attain," as you say. But why not write unconscious of *"the aim?"* Would not *the aim* be attained, and more happily? I ask, not to give, but to gain, information.

You hope companions are kind. These are favorite cousins. What a lovely spot this is! We are making a little sojourn of a week "in the beautiful valley." The Staubach is shimmering its long, filmy length in the sunlight to my right: the Jungfrau lifting just opposite its sun-struck dazzle of snow, and beautiful as she is reported, which cannot be said of all Jungfraus. The village is prettily scattered along the glacier stream "tearing like mad" through the depths of the valley; mountains hem it in, some snow-covered the year round; others, bare rock; lower ones are covered with trees and grass. Many show only precipitous walls, down which tumble and foam countless cascades. One long, wide reach of the mountain side is a vast meadow, here and there broken into knolls outlined by rows of trees, but the meadow part is mantled with the velvetiest green eyes ever fastened upon, and it is all dotted with little huts and barns, the lower half white and the upper, the richest reddish brown, under its roof of the same hue projecting into the deep eaves, we know so well from our ornamental "Swiss châlets." Nothing could be lovelier or more unique and picturesque. I have seen nothing equal to it, anywhere else. Words cannot picture it, and I do not believe any artist could paint it.

L. G. C.

Lauterbrunnen, July 29, 1886.

ON THE NILE.

YOU will have to take jostle instead of penmanship; but I have a comforting conviction that will be preferred to nothing at all, especially as I am giving you my best.

This is my third day's steaming up the Nile. The most enthusiastic tourists consider this prosaic in the extreme, and that the *dahabeah* is the only method by which to take the Nile. As for me—is it my accumulating years, I wonder?—I am more than content to be prosaic. We are about 125 or 130 miles from Cairo. Such a strange, kaleidoscopic, fascinating experience as this is! I think I have quite lost my head. I am totally unequal to putting it into words. But I shall try to toss you bits of it— Esterhazy scattering diamonds as he passes, if you choose! First, the thrilling episode. We steamed away from Marseilles "in the teeth of a storm," which rapidly grew into such violence even Miss B—— got to her prayers. For myself, I was in my berth, too sick—*i. e.,* dizzy— to care for anything. A tremendous wave burst through my door, flooding everything; the floor looked the very sea itself. I could lift my head only long enough to ask if the door was gone.

This was a dangerous storm indeed. No vessel left Marseilles for two days after ours on account of it. But we weathered it, and lived to enjoy the beautiful Mediterranean, the exceeding wonder of its blueness and its lovely sunrises and sunsets. Also, we made acquaintance with many pleasant fellow-passengers, and Miss B——, as is her wont, had a lively flirtation with a distinguished fellow-citizen from the Hub, now an appointee of government at Alexandria, "an associate justice of international law," or something like it.

We had a day at Alexandria. Saw one of the "seven wonders" it boasts of—the Pharos, Pompey's Pillar, the Serapeum, some of its bazaars, and had two charming drives to its famous quais and one garden. Everywhere all the phases of oriental life greeted us. Anything more exciting is inconceivable. Any enumeration would be absurd, as you know just what they must have been.

At dark the judge saw us off and looked a "Melancholy Jaques" indeed, as my detective eyes saw his parting pressure of Miss B—'s hand.

We came by train to Cairo. Such a charming young Englishman sat beside me, a naval officer. We fell into the friendliest talk at once, and kept it up until I was breathless. I saw him once again. We shook hands and parted. I do not know his name, but I shall remember him forever. I have come to think young English naval officers a class set apart; for at supper, on reaching the hotel, another sat beside me, and we talked till both forgot to "do justice to the fare before us." We met several times, and I have the most precious little good-by note which I shall never part with. At the second interview we merrily introduced each to the other. Do you know it makes my heart sore to think we shall never meet again?

The above is proof that after all the living human interest is paramount. The Cairo life into which I plunged, or maybe it swallowed me up, did not dim the tenderness of this experience.

At the Pyramids I would have written to you, but I found myself in the hands of the Philistines—Beduoins, and never did I enjoy anything more. Beyond all the wonder, sublimity of feeling and unutterable admiration for them, the Pyramids, another of the seven—came a curious thrill of bond and blood that made me sit down with and walk about with, "that throng of importunate vendors of spurious antiques," and try to get at them. Shrewd, amiable, bright, ready, handsome, picturesque-looking fellows—we were soon on the best of terms. We *gripped* hands at parting. No, the devil is not as black as he is painted! They made Miss B— nervous. But I hope I shall see them again.

Also we saw the lone pillar at Heliopolis, a garden in which is the "Virgin's tree"—I have leaves and a ball from it; it is a syacmore—an *ostrich garden* with 600 of the bare-legged bypeds strutting round and now and then flapping their $300 apiece matchless feathers. The Museum, where mummies "are a drug," and genuine scarabea too, but you could not buy one of them for "a mint of money." The island of Rhoda, where Pharaoh's daughter picked up Moses. The indescribable mosques, tombs of the Khalifs, Bachas and Marmelukes, and just a thousand or more wonders that seemed to have been handed down from the "Arabian

ON THE NILE. 299

Nights." Camels, donkeys, turbaned Turks, Nubians blacker than night, veiled women—I can more easily tell you what was not than what was there. I am only sorry I cannot go back and stay "ever so long." Six days—that is only an aggravation!

The steamer lands at every point of interest, and arrangements are made for us to see them. Donkeys and camels where too far to walk. We went on donkeys to see the site of Memphis, Tombs of Apis and the Serapum, etc. My donkey and its little sixteen year old driver were jewels. The first was as well gaited as any horse, and the latter was proud to show him off—too proud to take any account of his own sixteen mile trot. All we saw at Memphis was the site of some fragments of statues and temples. The shifting sands sometimes bury it from sight; sometimes, but rarely, leave a little bare. The tombs are in splendid order for seeing; long avenues, the floor a perfect level, and everybody carrying a candle. You can fancy how unique and beautiful the flitting glimmer of the moving throng—now peering into the dark recesses in which are the great, massive tombs, or again running their lights along the walls to see the exquisite picture stones, or gathering in groups to discuss them. But oh! how I wish all I care for could see with their own eyes!

As we glide along, we see many characteristic features of this "twelve miles wide" strip of wonderland. Long trains of camels; Bedouin encampments; stately fellows in white turbans and flowing draperies, sweeping past on their fleet steeds; vast green fields; mud towns and villages; the tall, beautiful palms in groves and avenues; sugar plantations, with their stacked canes and great factories; long tongues of sand fringed with pelicans; flocks of herons winging their way in the blue sky; and—there is the luncheon gong!

After that interesting collation, how tiresome eating is! I wish we could live on air, perfume of flowers, sunbeams and the like. Everybody nearly is English, and they come out strong as trenchermen and women. One, Canon Farrer, not *the* canon of Westminster, eats and drinks to—well, it is none of my business. I need see nothing. I do not wish to. The "guests" of this steamer number ex-members of Parliament and their families, canons, curates, and plenty of people with "handles to their names;" but they are not specially interesting. Mr. Cook owns these steamers and is himself aboard — a large, rather fine-looking man, but far from being a model of deportment; simply seems quite deficient in good manners.

The river, the land, the people, the animals, the ruins and their history, and legends with books, books forever! furnish my daily food. But I like companionship, and if the whole truth must be told prefer that of some really "splendid man" to this of my own sex. One can live too much in books, I fear. Do not they unfit for

> "Living in common ways with
> Common men?"

But why should I complain of anything under the sun?

Well, good-bye.

L. G. C.

On the Nile, December 30, 1886.

EGYPT (FROM PARIS).

NOTHING like agreeable surprises, is there? I ought to be on the broad Atlantic, but am not. Let Miss B—— go without me several days ago. I am going to linger here for several weeks longer. There is the woman for you! I wonder if I can go back to where I left off. What did I tell you? I wish I could recall. But don't you call my young naval officers "infernal." I cannot allow that. If only you could have seen and known them, you would go down on your knees to take that back. You cannot even know how sore it makes my heart to think I shall never see them again. Ah! woe is me!

No, I did not, "of course, take a run over to Jerusalem." Yet two more weeks would have accomplished that. The other two, Miss B—— and her friend, would not even consider it. I could not go alone. But indeed Egypt was enough, had we only stayed long enough. What we had was for me that "first taste of blood that makes the tiger." Did I not tell you

I had found out what it was to be a "lotus-eater?"

No need of anything but sitting still to be borne by that invisible, noiseless steam-power up and down the Nile—that wonderful, mysterious, enchanted stream. How its waters—your warning came too late; I had already quaffed deep and long of it—thank the Lord if that take me back!—slipped away from beneath us; how the banks studded here with its picture-villages built of mud, there with groves of stately palm trees, or yonder with some famous ruins, sped by carrying the enraptured gaze with them into the distances that dimmed and melted into the sky; how the unfolding scenes ahead won it after a time of dreams, revery, ecstasy, to behold great hills gliding towards us with lengthening chains of grottoes hewed out of their solid rock, and wrought and carved into stately monuments for dead kings or their mighty subjects; how the day wore on to sunsets of inexpressible glory, succeeded by intervals of curious grey, and then—the sudden afterglow that made sky, air, water and earth an ethereal commingling of "all the tints that in the colors of the rainbow live and play in the plighted clouds!" Ah! mere existence there was bliss, more than akin, beyond that of lotus-eating. But alas! how to give you any idea of it!

There was a comical side, or else I must have become a slave to the enchantment of such a life. The contact with the natives. They came in swarms the moment the steamer landed, to beg if there was no excursion; with their donkeys to act as "guides" if there was. Here is an instance: We were to go to the rock tombs of Beni-Hassan. At seven in the morning, behold me mounted on a miserable little scrap of a donkey, for which my English saddle even more than myself was a world too large. The road varied from sharp inclines to steep ascents. How was I to stick to my steed, was scarcely queried before I found myself clasped in the dirty arms of my tall Arab and firmly pinioned. No use to squirm. That only made him tighten his embrace. My only comfort was seeing all my sisters in the same plight. I do not know what I did not dread; but certainly hosts to which your Holy Land of "f——s" would have been welcome guests. Once at the tombs, I forgot my terrors. Spacious chambers hollowed out of the solid rock, with ceiling and walls decorated with biographical

EGYPT, FROM PARIS.

paintings; all the details of the history of the life of the occupant. And in front those magnificent columns "that have preceded our era, notwithstanding their Doric appearance, by some 3,000 years," says Mariette Bey. They *are* perfect Doric style, and imposing as magnificent. One of the pictures is that of a body of emigrants, "the most ancient-known example of the hordes attracted by the proverbial fertility of Egypt." Its date is 4,800 years ago. Three days and a half at Luxor and Karnak and Thebes. Temples, kings, tombs, palaces, Colossi-obelisks, all carved in intaglios and reliefs, and covered with those brilliant paintings that defy time, weather, everything but the profaning hand of man. I rode to melodious Memnon on a donkey *in a shower*. Rain in Egypt! And it was afternoon! Bah! how I detest doing the right thing at the wrong time. I thought of you and the letter I meant to have written on that lofty knee. I had my music, though!

All the way to the limit of my trip, Assuan, "ancient Syene," there was repetition of landings, donkeys, guides, rides and ruins. I never tired. Each had its special attractions. I lived in a daze. Ah! I wish every time I think of them to be back and doing it all over and over again. Yes, when I come, you *must* listen and *look*. For I shall have pictures to help me tell their story—those beautiful, sublime monuments of a mighty people and civilization, vanished from the face of the earth these thousands of years ago.

I am growing eager to see that "Venture on the Sea of Literature." Have I told you I like the title amazingly? I shall be astonished and disgusted if it is not a happy hit. It shall be! Those— Your friend,

L. G. C.

Paris, February 10, 1883.

CUBA.

YES, I went to Cuba, and it was a ravishing experience. Not quite an Eden, but so near to being! There was not an American (*i. e.,* a Yankee) of us all who did not fully believe it *would be,* once "Uncle Sam" held it in his sturdy grip. To the last man and woman and the best, we defiantly broke the commandment and coveted our neighbor's possession with our whole hearts. It is the most unreal reality, the most dream-like substantiality, the most vision-like, sure-enough scrap of earth imaginable. I feared to shut my eyes, lest on opening them it would have vanished. It looked as magical an isle as that. Oh—h! Just writing about it makes me catch my breath and widen my eyes to get it all back again.

The unspeakable splendors of its tropical vegetation—not only avenues and groves of "lofty palm trees," but vast forests of them; not only "lofty palm trees," but countless others, gorgeous in a burst of bloom without foliage—not a suspicion of green mingled with that blaze of richest rose, scarlet, purple or white, as it happened to be; not trees only, but clambering vines, all aflower with such lily bells as made me rub my eyes to make sure there was no illusion; and oh! such vistas and vistas of "the wonders of creation" as made me marvel what surpassing them could be possible in any other sphere!

I wish you could have seen the sunrise as we steamed into the harbor of Havana, the city itself seeming to rise out of the water like "beautiful Venice," and like it, fashioned by the cunningest conjury out of sunbeams, the colors of the rainbow, the ethereal elements of the blue empyrean, the crystalline layers of the atmosphere, the tints of time and the films of earth! Yes, and have stood, as I stood later, on the ramparts of the fort, taking in such a spectacle of "the kingdoms of this earth" as swept me into thinking it almost equaled that of the Great Temptation on the Mount!

I am forgetting to tell you of the trip. We took the steamer Niagara at St. Augustine. It was fresh and clean and very comfortable. Among our fellow-travelers were several who proved very companionable and courteous. The weather was bright, mild, delightful. There were several young Cubans, quite attractive in appearance.

Next morning I rose early and went on deck in time for the sunrise. It was wonderful. The "First Officer" said, "It is a rare sunrise," which made me more than thankful to see it. After breakfast, I stayed on deck to see the gulf sights. Saw jelly-fish in great numbers; they looked like fungi. The coast of Florida was in sight all the time; also an occasional vessel, ship or steamer. At night, Cape Farewell light-house, the long wake of gleaming, flashing phosphorescent waves; Orion, in all his glory overhead, and the stars more brilliant than I had ever seen them. Remained up so late did not undress, as I wished to be on deck again at the earliest possible hour. At 5:30 the moon was in its last quarter; the sky a lovely glow. Just as the sun rose above the horizon, we were steaming into port. The spectacle was indescribably beautiful and unique. Fort Morro Castle, on its not high bluff, the circular sweep of the shore line, the city as it were rising out of the water, with its buildings so varied in size, style and color; the harbor filled with shipping and innumerable little craft shooting hither and thither, and the dazzling sunlight firing it all into a glory no words could catch!

We were quickly passed into a rude kind of gondola, and skimmed over the liquid interval between the steamer and quai.

What a medley of fellow-beings awaited us on landing! What a jargon of sounds! Everything so new and strange to us. A procession of cabs and victorias bore us our several ways. We went to Hotel Quinta Menida, kept by a young fellow-countryman in conjunction with some Cubans. The building is in the Moresque style, round a triangular court, arcades on this court to two stories. The entrance on the ground floor is under an arcade that goes round the entire exterior, into a lofty vestibule like those seen all over Europe. This ground floor is paved with great slabs of stone! the stairways and all the other floors with white marble. The ceilings are from eighteen to twenty feet high. Windows and doors are also very high and broad. On the halls there are double doors, a massive inside one, and a glazed outside one of half its height. This is for ventilation and privacy. The same massive doors open on the balconies with which every room is provided and the outer with marble slats, for adjusting the light. The two middle panes of the inner doors are on hinges, making them movable for the same purpose. There are no glass windows such as we have, but there are transoms in ornamental devices of stained glass, generally white and blue. The house has three stories, and a flat roof with a balustrade that can be used for promenading or sitting. The laundry is on one corner, and Chinese, blacks, children and dogs seem to be perfectly at home there. The view was fine and extensive.

We went over the whole edifice, peering into the rooms, corridors, etc., getting that "first *lasting* impression." The parlor is an immense room, furnished peculiarly, one-half being in cane seat, sofas and chairs placed in the wall! Rows of flowers all around; a central rug, with a geometrical square of rocking chairs inclosing it, and a table in the center. In the exact center of the spacious room, another table, with a fixed number of chairs packed up close to it. On the opposite side, the same arrangement is reproduced in upholstered furniture, covered with white Holland. From the ceiling depended chandeliers and brackets of tropical blooms and vines, while the side walls were covered with great mirrors. The entire interior is white. As a room, it is certainly unique. I have never seen anything like it. The arcades on this parlor floor are full of small tables, where the meals are served, of which there are two, breakfast at 9 a. m. and dinner at 6 p. m. The dishes are the same for both, except the addition of soup for dinner. Oranges caught on a fork and peeled—it takes both practice and skill to accomplish this—are sucked, the pulp not being swallowed. Fried plantains are a disappointment, tasting as if they had soured before or in the process of cooking. A small panfish is exceedingly delicate and appetizing, and a very petite banana is delicious. Coffee is only tolerable. Can any anywhere compare with our own "home coffee?" Ice is manufactured and the supply is abundant.

One of the first things to do was to take an orientation drive. The temperature was perfect; a breeze, just warm enough, just cool enough, blowing steadily. The sky was tinted in pinks, green and gold. The city seemed an enchanted one. I half feared to close my eyes, lest it would vanish. The houses had caught the sky tints, being "in all the colors of the rainbow;" are painted so. The most of them are but one story or two stories. Arcades are the rule, some with columns of different color from the house. The windows, almost without exception, are unglazed, having instead a light iron grating. This is a most singular and curious feature. The inmates chat through them with friends on the outside, looking as if in prison. Mischievous or "venturesome" urchins clamber up and cling to the inside like birds in a cage. The Prado, quite recently laid out, and many of the squares, are beautiful and light up brilliantly in the very superior quality of gas. The streets were not thronged, as I expected them to be. There was a glorious "afterglow," which gave us as long a drive as we wished. I got up at 2 a. m. to look for the Southern Cross, that same "First Officer" having told me it did not rise till after midnight. I saw it, to my great gratification. This was the second time. The first time was on the Nile.

One morning, we went out early "to go to market," this being "a thing to do" in all cities of note. The walk was short, leading past one of the public squares, with few trees, but pleasant looking. There was a most miscellaneous crowd of people and "beasts of burden." Horses (very small) and donkeys with immense panniers filled with every conceivable product and commodity; *tows* of them fastened to each other by their tails, and so covered up with their burdens only their feet were visible. Fancy the spectacle. The women were of the common and lowest classes, dark-yellow and black in color, wearing no bonnets, of course, but only some light veil over the head. Very few of either men or women looked clean. The market building was a large structure, well lighted, and exhibiting every known vegetable as well as all the delicious tropical fruits.

I had an experience worth chronicling. My watch was in its little outside breast-pocket attached by pin and chain, but in full view. A fine, open-countenanced man at one of the stalls touched me gently on my arm and warned me to put it out of sight. This was done in pantomine, as he spoke no English and I no Spanish, but was as "plain as words could say it." I never felt or gave warmer thanks. The dirt and odors soon became unbearable, and we returned to our hotel just in time for breakfast.

We tried a shopping expedition with some other ladies and an interpreter—a very pretty Cuban—but it was not a success. Saw nothing characteristic but the mode of shopping.

The goods were brought to our carriages and shown to us by the interpreter and a clerk.

One afternoon we went to the Cathedral; it was grey and rather picturesque, but what we wished to see was not shown, so we soon left. Thence we drove to the Gov.-General's country-seat to see its noted garden, which went beyond expectation. We walked through avenues of stately palms, and saw tropical trees in bloom of which we had never read or heard. One, the Carolinas, had fringe-like tassels of blossoms in Magenta color, graduated from very deep to the faintest tint. The threadlike fringe was tipped with the deepest red and gold. This was one of those "without foliage or a suspicion of green." The house is unpretending indeed, and the grounds only fairly kept up. Brought away several flowers and pressed them.

After our 6 o'clock dinner and a short reunion in the parlor, a party of us went to one of the most frequented of the public squares to hear the band and watch the crowd. The party consisted of a German gentleman from Chicago, of political and journal prominence, a Catholic priest from New England—his tongue shot with such arrows of wit and flashes of eloquence one could hardly keep back a "hurra! for old Ireland!" and two ladies beside myself. I fell to the care of the priest, and made merry over having a priest for a cavalier, as I took his arm. But indeed it was a curious experience.

We found seats and watched the kaleidoscopic show. One feature claimed special attention—the way the men and women kept apart. This is not more pronounced in a Quaker meeting-house. The priest pointed out the son of the Duke of Leeds, a tall, large, striking-looking man and a count. Indeed, the graphic, lively loquacity of the good "Father" added so much to our entertainment, we included him *nolens volens* in all our after movements. At 9:30 we went to a grand café and had lemonade, milk punch and wine. Oh! I must not forget to tell you my gallant escort presented me with a bouquet.

Next day we went to Cerro, a suburb of fine private residences with an "aristocratic convent." We drove up to one of the handsomest places, and got permission to walk through it. This proved to be the residence of the Senator to Spain. His young son escorted us, as well as the gardener, and both were models of courtesy. They presented us with flowers and leaves, among the latter being that of the guava, which I have pressed. We could only drive around the Convent of the Sacred Heart, not having provided ourselves with any introduction. We gained admission to another residence, that of a Senor de la Costa. It and its grounds were a dream of beauty. But I must to other excursions, or I will never get away from Cuba.

One to a great sugar plantation—a charming drive from the city. This was under the auspices of the German gentleman, who had letters of introduction to everything worth seeing in the island. When we reached the entrance gate, admission was most decidedly denied. It took talk and time to obtain even an interview with the owner. Finally he came—a very handsome, young, distingue-looking man. At first he was most haughtily courteous and immovable—*could not grant entrance.* A recent experience with some ill-mannered fellow-countrymen finally explained this. In the absence of the family, they had gone into the house, invaded every part of it, despite the remonstrances of the servants. At last he gave way and at once became the most gracious of hosts, treating us as if we were specially invited guests. He went with us himself through all the works, showing and explaining, and we saw the full process of the sugar-making, from the feeding of the stalks to the mills to where it came forth in beautiful glittering crystals of golden-brown sugar. On parting, he presented each with a cornucopia of it, filled by himself in our presence. I shall keep mine intact as long as I live.

Another took in two plantations—one of bananas, the other of pineapples. We had the privilege of gathering from each for ourselves. A very small bunch of bananas sufficed, and we had them put in our carriages while we walked some distance to the pineapple plantation. None of us had ever seen one. It belonged to some native Cubans who had a cottage at the entrance. One went with us as guide. The plants were in regular rows, averaging from four to five feet in height, one apple to each rising in the center of a large cluster of stiff leaves that curve like those of the aloe, and have much the same appearance and coloring. The guide invited us to pluck for ourselves, each took one. We little suspected what "a big contract" even one was, as we gayly and proudly started on the return tramp, after having tried to see which could find *the biggest one* to pluck. Shifting back and forth, first one hand and then the other, began almost immediately. This did not help long. In a very few moments I was lagging and panting, and next, possessed with a fright and dread that the arms could not hold out and that I would have to drop my treasure. Then such a jump of my heart! A quick step by my side, a relieving hand slipped between mine and that stem held by such a despairing clutch, and voice and words that might have been those of my own special "good angel:" "Allow me to carry your apple." But didn't I! At the cottage, a feast of pineapples awaited us—peeled, sliced and laid in sugar-besprinkled layers. "Fit food for the gods" indeed! I wonder if they ever had such.

Just one more excursion, and I will have to sing:

"Beautiful isle, farewell, farewell."

This was to the caves, sixty miles by rail from Havana. A very early start was imperative, so we were at the station before it was clear dawn and partaking of a breakfast of coffee and rolls to serve the sixty miles. It was far from being a temptation to over-indulgence! The cave was a short drive from the railway and was made in a variety of vehicles; but the day was fine and our spirits elastic, and every moment seemed a special enjoyment, in spite of our lack of comfort. The cave itself awoke all our enthusiasm. Up pretty ascents, down into twilight depths, across fairy-like bridges, among subterranean wonders that exhausted exclamations, and panting and perspiring till my escort, the German gentleman, groaned between gasps, "I didn't bargain for this!" Fortunately, at that juncture, we came upon one of the most extraordinary features, a large, magnificent, perfectly-formed organ. Striking it brought forth sonorous responses. A kind of awe hushed us into silence. The Bride, another of these extraordinary formations, next elicited unlimited admiration. She stood, gowned in white, with her filmy veil enveloping her, as if waiting for the bridegroom. By what subtle processes of congelation had nature fashioned anything so realistic! One could only gaze and question, and give homage, and leaving her presence, turn to look again and again, not hoping to see her ever again.

Do you wonder we were loath to leave the beautiful island? I said, "I have always been opposed to annexation, but Cuba! Yes, I own to wishing for it henceforth."

I think I have never imposed a postscript on you. Now I am going to.

Looking over what I have written, I find I have omitted mentioning one thing of great moment. It seems that many of the planters are retaining in slavery a number of colored people who are really free, but ignorant of the fact. These, I presume, are the ones who come under the decree giving freedom to all slaves sixty or over sixty years old, issued by the Spanish government July, 1870. This is surely a crying injustice.

L. G. C.

Cuba, April 7, 1885.

A VISION OF FATIGUE.

WE were a party of nine or ten, making a summer of it.

Put-in-Bay came first on the list of places to be visited. It was unusually crowded and brilliant that season. All the hotels were full. The weather was enchanting; the temperature exhilarating. Even the wines for which it was so celebrated were not more so. Day after day sped in a kind of intoxication till we felt we could bear it no longer, and to the last one of us voted to go home for a rest!

That trip was one to be remembered. It was Sunday afternoon. We had to take an excursion steamer, on boarding which the only "standing-room" even to be had was to lean against the pillars of the deck. After a long wait—taking turns—in this way, the captain had his state-room put at our service, and we realized what a gift of an invention chairs were. On reaching our home port at 2:30 a. m., we had to trudge several miles, sharing the carrying of twin babies with their two nurses. No one complained or shirked. But the lines—

> "—bed —bed—delicious bed,
> That heaven or earth to the weary head,"

were never more convincing than when we sought ours.

Next morning breakfast at nine, and an immediate return to them.

At once, on dragging and throwing myself upon mine, the vision began.

I was back at Put-in-Bay. It was a crystal world. The island, hotels, houses, people, the distant shores with their villages, the various vessels, all, everything, I could see in and through, as I floated around in a lovely little sail-boat of crystal, and looked down through its bottom into the crystal depths of the lake.

But there was no time to be lost in wonder. In the twinkling of an eye, I was standing in space surrounded by gigantic mountains that rose to the very firmament. They were of countless shapes, some cloven into rifts and clefts, others smooth as velvet lawns, and so precipitous I felt what the dizziness would be to dare to look down. Presently my gaze was fixed by one just in front of me. There was a monstrous fissure in which, carved as it were, was a giant knee, slightly crooked or bent. Years before I had read the anecdote about Cuvier; his positive conviction and assertion that fossil man would be found, and his reply when asked from time to time, "*pas encore.*" I exclaimed under my breath: "Why, there is Cuvier's fossil man." In a breath I was in a subterranean chamber of vast proportions, with lofty ceiling and octagonal in shape. The walls were studded with the richest jewels, and it was lighted by a soft yet clear radiance—an opaline mist of exquisite tints. At intervals were placed large caskets on pedestals, these, too, incrusted with gems.

On my approaching, in succession, one after another, some unseen agency lifted each cover, revealing all the most celebrated stones I had ever read of. The Kohinoor lay in a dull mass on a velvet cushion. The green diamond flashed into tempered light. Orlaff shone as it might have if it ever was the eye of an Indian idol. The Regent blazed till I could look no longer. Suddenly such a lovely brilliant! "Oh! this is the Great Rosy diamond of the fairy story I read so long ago!" I cried, bending over eagarly. To find myself seated on a throne of mother-of-pearl, and being borne onward by some invisible force, swift as light, through an arcade of sea-shells. "Why, this is like Bayard Taylor's arcade of rainbows—as beautiful! as beautiful!" I commented. Shells such as I had never seen, different in shape, color and luster, but uniform in size, were fitted together from a height far overhead to a depth far below. On and on, dazzled, enchanted, bewildered, yet commenting without pause, till I was gazing, transfixed, on such a spectacle as would have lifted the apocalyptic John into the Seventh Heaven!

Then rose before me Jerusalem on its hill, the holy city of the Jews, with its sacred temple, the city of the Crusades, the city of pilgrimages, the city of the New Testament. And beyond and above it, the heavens were opened, and the New Jerusalem was revealed in all the glory of its prophecies, traditions and beliefs. The Promise and the Fulfillment! Awe-struck, almost blinded, I was gazing from one to the other, saying to myself: "How can I ever describe what I have seen? How explain it? Where find words to express it? There is nothing, nothing, I can compare it to or with"—

A repeated tapping at my door, which I heard but could make no response to. Then I knew the maid had gone away. Presently, another rap; then the door unclosed and my name called; finally, a touch and gentle shaking roused me as if from a nightmare. It was half-past two. I had not lost consciousness for a moment, but I had not moved or spoken aloud. When I described the above to a learned friend, he said it was caused by the preceding extreme fatigue. I accepted the explanation.

www.ingramcontent.com/pod-product-compliance
Lightning Source LLC
Chambersburg PA
CBHW030401230426
43664CB00007BB/693